JUNIOR GREAT BOOKS®

Read-Aloud Program

Teacher's Edition

Pegasus Series

The Great Books Foundation

A nonprofit educational organization

Copyright © 1990 by The Great Books Foundation

Chicago, Illinois

All rights reserved

ISBN 978-0-945159-96-4

9   8

Printed in the United States of America

Published and distributed by

The Great Books Foundation

A nonprofit educational organization

35 East Wacker Drive, Suite 400

Chicago, IL 60601

www.greatbooks.org

SFI Certified Sourcing
www.sfiprogram.org
SFI-00453

PEGASUS SERIES

TEACHER'S EDITION

Welcome to the Junior Great Books® Read-Aloud program. This program will give your students continuous opportunities to interact with excellent literature and to develop their reading, writing, oral communication, and interpretive-thinking skills. The Read-Aloud program bridges the gap between children's real capacity to think interpretively about literature and their limited decoding skills. The program enables *all* your students—both nonreaders and experienced readers—to think about and actively respond to high-quality literature.

Each unit in the Pegasus Series consists of a story or group of three poems, and a set of interpretive activities for four thirty-minute classroom sessions and an at-home session (to be completed with an adult partner). Concentrating on each selection in this way gives all children the time and the means to comprehend a rich work of literature fully, to learn from each other, and to work out their own individual perspectives.

As your class participates in the program, they will learn to communicate their ideas about the selections by exercising the whole range of language skills needed to become good readers. The children's Read-Aloud books are designed to help students practice these skills in very concrete ways—through drawing, making notes, discussing interpretive questions, and writing questions of their own. Students are also able to personalize the stories and poems through artwork and writing as they record their individual responses in their books. Throughout each unit, children can review their work in order to refresh or revise their thinking, or perhaps just to take pride in the body of work they have produced.

As in Junior Great Books for older children, you have the distinctive role of Shared Inquiry™ leader, helping students work together to find meaning in a work and to build interpretations. To fill this role, your personal curiosity about the selections, and an active interest in each child's ideas, are the best teaching equipment. As you work with the stories and poems and become familiar with the various interpretive issues in each selection, your ability to help students communicate their thoughts and develop their ideas will increase. You will also find that as you lead more Read-Aloud units, both you and your students will become more adept at exploring the issues contained in each story or group of poems.

The following introduction will give you the guidance needed to conduct the Read-Aloud program in a whole-class setting. Included are suggestions for tailoring the various activities to meet your individual classroom needs. The Read-Aloud schedule itself is meant to be flexible, and it may be adapted to suit your class size and schedule, as well as your students' skill levels. You will also find suggestions for encouraging parental involvement in the at-home portion of the program, and recommendations for recruiting parent volunteers to help out in the classroom. If you are looking for ways to integrate Read-Aloud themes into other subject areas, such as social studies, science, and math, you will find suggested topics in Appendix D.

CONTENTS

YOUR PREPARATION

Prepare for the Read-Aloud program as you would normally prepare to lead Junior Great Books: read the selection through twice, taking notes as you read, and then write—ideally with a colleague—your own interpretive questions.

Since oral presentation of a literary text is central to the program, it might be a good idea to practice reading the selection aloud, so that your listeners will get the full benefit of its unique language and of your own interest and enjoyment. In particular, you may want to rehearse the poetry and those stories with a very distinctive style, such as "The Pied Piper" and "The Mermaid Who Lost Her Comb." However, because of the quality of the Read-Aloud selections, simply being responsive to the natural rhythm of the writing and the language itself should ensure an effective oral reading.

All of the selections in the Read-Aloud program have been carefully chosen for their emotional and imaginative appeal as well as their thematic appropriateness for young children. But it is natural that you will connect more readily with some selections than with others. Should you have difficulty connecting with a story or poem, you may want to take some additional time in your preparation to familiarize yourself with the text and to think over the interpretive issues suggested in the activities. You'll find that these selections will come alive when children offer their ideas and reactions. Sharing their curiosity and interest will richly repay your extra efforts.

Read the overview and the specific directions for each unit's activities, so that you can plan the week's schedule and anticipate any adaptations you may want to make or any materials you may need to prepare in advance. You might also want to refer to Appendix D for a list of additional readings, and for suggested ways to integrate Read-Aloud themes into other areas of your curriculum.

P R O G R A M   R O U T I N E

When you begin your Read-Aloud program, you will want to tell students some of the things that distinguish this program from their other classroom work. Let children know that each week they will be hearing a story or poem read several times, and they will be talking about it with each other. They will be thinking about and asking a lot of different questions, including special ones called *interpretive questions*. Interpretive questions are special because they have more than one good answer.

Tell children, too, that their Read-Aloud books are special because they will get to draw in the important pictures themselves. In this way, every person's book will be unique, reflecting how each of us sees the story in our own mind. (If children wonder why the pictures in the books are in black and white, you can tell them that *they* will be supplying the color, because their drawings are the important ones.)

SESSION I

• Introducing the Story or Poem
We often give you a brief introduction that is meant to orient students or to provide a necessary definition or reference. For example, we suggest that you tell students that "pied" means "having patches or spots of many colors" and that a "piper" is someone who plays a flute or pipe, so they can visualize the main character of "The Pied Piper."

It is possible that to meet the needs of your class you will have to add to the recommended introductions. However, we suggest that you keep introductions brief, so as not to diminish the anticipation of the first reading.

• The First Reading
The first reading of a selection gives children the opportunity to experience a rich work of literature without the obstacle of difficult decoding. Listening to the unimpeded flow of a narrative, children are able to react on both an imaginative and emotional level, and all begin their interpretive work on a selection on an equal footing. You will find that even very skilled readers appreciate hearing a good story or poem read aloud.

At first, you might need to experiment a little to see what type of environment is best suited for reading aloud to your class. Ideally, readings should be intimate, with children sitting in a group around you (perhaps in assigned places), so that all can clearly hear the story or poem and see the pictures.

As you read, have children listen without referring to their books. There will be opportunities for children to follow along in their books during the second and third readings.

Keep interruptions during your first reading to a minimum since children will have a chance to ask questions when you are finished. Don't feel you need to define every unfamiliar word for children. Many vocabulary items add to the flavor of the work but are not crucial to understanding, and it is preferable not to break the flow of the reading. Nor is the asking of prediction questions appropriate for this reading. Such questions lead children to speculate about what the author will specifically address—and in Shared Inquiry, children are encouraged not to guess, but to base their opinions on the text. You will want to pause and show the pictures, however, since they often depict scenes and objects that will aid children in understanding the story or poem.

• Sharing First Responses

This brief, informal exchange after the first reading of a selection allows children time to clear up any misunderstandings or factual errors. At the same time, it encourages an atmosphere in which children learn that different opinions and reactions are an important part of thinking about literature. This sharing time also allows children to see that their initial responses can provide the seeds of original ideas that are worth ongoing reflection.

After the first reading, allow five minutes or so to clear up any confusion children might have had about the story or poem. Ask them if they have any questions, and answer—or have the class answer—the factual questions. If children ask interpretive questions (which they will do naturally, especially after they have done a few units) do not engage in a lengthy discussion. Children will be far better prepared to address such questions after they have heard the selection read a few more times. Instead, tell the class that you think an interpretive question has been asked, and that they will want to think about it during the course of the week.

Children might not have any questions about the story, but they probably will have some definite reactions. Always encourage students to voice their opinions by asking them what parts of the story or poem they especially liked and why.

• The First Art Activity

The first session generally ends with an art activity, which serves as closure to the session and gives children the opportunity to record their early responses to the selection. Activities include drawing a favorite part of a story, illustrating a memorable scene or image, or noting an important pattern in the text through small sketches called art notes.

Refer to the specific assignments. Occasionally, you will want to ask a few questions or have children share some ideas to help them get started on their drawings. See each unit's instruction pages for suggested questions.

AT-HOME WORK

This second reading of the selection gives children the opportunity to internalize the facts of the story or poem at a pace suited to their individual comprehension levels. In the comfortable and intimate one-on-one environment of the at-home reading, children are also able to respond more personally and thoughtfully to a selection. When discussing a story or poem at home, without the social pressures of the classroom, children feel freer to try out ideas and often do some of their most creative thinking. After students have developed some answers, and have practiced saying them out loud to another person, they are ready to continue the more formal work of the classroom with increased confidence.

When you send the Read-Aloud books home, be sure children understand what they are to do with their parents: listen as their parents read, follow along if they can, and repeat or join in saying the underlined phrases. Point out the "G.B." character and tell children that whenever they see it, they are to pause and discuss the question in the box, and mark the text if asked to do so. Finally, they are to write or dictate their "My Question"—asking about anything in the text they wondered about—in the space provided at the end of the selection. If you feel children need a model for the kind of question to ask, think back to what they said after the first reading, formulate some questions, and write a few examples on the board. Do not feel that children's "My Questions" must be interpretive. Any question children have about the selection should be respected. Make sure students understand that the drawing assignments and the other writing assignments will be done at school. (If children are interested in G.B.'s name, tell them, or see if they can guess, that the character's initials come from the program they are participating in—*Great Books*.)

SESSION 2

• Posting "My Questions"
Displaying students' "My Questions" in a prominent place emphasizes the idea that each child's curiosity about a selection is worth considering and pursuing. Posting these questions fosters the idea of Shared Inquiry by communicating respect for each child's contribution to the group effort to understand works of literature. And as children see the questions of their classmates and point out their own questions, their reading comprehension is also bolstered.

The day after reading the selection with the at-home reader, students cut out their questions and pin them on a special Sharing Questions bulletin board. (Children who have not had an at-home reading can dictate their questions to you at this time.) Each week you might want to add the title of the unit to the bulletin board and have children decorate the board according to the unit's theme.

Tell students that they will be thinking about their questions during the next few days and discussing some of them in the Sharing Questions Discussion at the end of the week. In a few instances, a unit has no Sharing Questions Discussion, but children should still be encouraged to look at each other's questions and to listen to see if their questions are asked during the other activities.

You will want to make use of students' questions while conducting activities during the week. For instance, if a number of children ask a question that you believe is factual, you might want to address it early on. Also check to see if children's questions fall into any groupings; you may want to shape activities to pick up on their shared curiosity.

Another way to use children's questions is to cross-reference them with the textual analysis and suggested follow-up questions printed in the margins of your text, seeing if any children posed similar ones. Then, whenever possible, use the children's versions, mentioning their names. Or, introduce your question by saying that it is related to the questions asked by such and such students.

• Reading and Review of G.B.'s Questions

The third reading focuses on further developing students' critical-thinking skills—building on children's initial reactions to a selection as well as on the interpretations initiated during the at-home work. With the basic facts of the story or poem clear, children can concentrate on a more thoughtful, interpretive reading of the selection as they discuss important passages with their classmates. Students come to understand that reading can be both a private and a shared experience, and that meaning is enriched when ideas are pursued and explored among a community of readers.

During this reading, have students try to follow along in their books as you read, and encourage them to join in saying the underlined words and phrases. Pause when you come to G.B.'s questions and collect students' responses. Pursue their answers with appropriate follow-up questions—in effect, engage in small Shared Inquiry discussions. The questions given in the margins of your text are meant to help you develop children's thoughts about the selection. But, of course, the students' comments are the best source for your follow-up questions.

REMAINDER OF SESSION 2; SESSION 3; SESSION 4

The variety of individual and group activities created for each selection reflects the fact that young children learn and express themselves in many different ways. Because of the unhurried pacing of the units, all children have the opportunity to display their strengths and discover new ones. All activities are interpretive in nature, and thus encourage students to think more deeply about their reactions to a story or poem and to develop their own ideas about it.

Read-Aloud activities for the later sessions include those that focus on meaningful vocabulary, dramatizations, and additional art activities. At some point during Session 3 or Session 4, you will lead an interpretive discussion, either a Sharing Questions Discussion or a textual analysis. After this discussion, children extend their experience with literature through group creative writing or individual compositions.

The rest of this introduction describes in detail the various Read-Aloud activities and offers guidance in how to conduct them.

INTERPRETIVE DISCUSSION

Throughout a Read-Aloud unit, children discuss their responses to the selection. But toward the end of the week, after they have expressed a variety of ideas, students are all the more prepared to build on their interpretations and come to conclusions through more formal discussion.

Sharing Questions Discussion is the culminating activity in most Read-Aloud units. It is similar to a Junior Great Books Shared Inquiry discussion, but is adapted for younger participants; it is shorter, and is based on a group of five or six interpretive questions, some of which children have contributed themselves. Your role as leader remains the same. By asking questions, you provide students with an example of a person intellectually engaged by literature.

Prepare to lead Sharing Questions Discussion by referring to the interpretive questions you wrote during your preparation and seeing if you have any to add. Then decide on the five or six questions you intend to ask your class. Note which of the children's "My Questions" are similar to the ones you plan to lead, and try to include three or four of their questions in your final list. Keep track of whose questions you use in Sharing Questions Discussion, since over the course of the semester you will want to make sure that each student has one of his or her questions mentioned at least once.

Sharing Questions Discussion will be more successful if the number of children participating is limited. Ten to fifteen children is an optimum number for discussion. A more intimate setting helps children concentrate on the questions and responses, and gives each child more opportunities to contribute ideas. If your class is large, consider dividing it into two groups. A parent volunteer can either lead one of the discussions, or conduct an activity (such as "My Favorite Words") with one group while you lead the other in discussion.

Begin Sharing Questions Discussion by writing your questions on the board, in the order you intend to ask them. (This practice will help children follow the discussion and focus on each question as it is being discussed.) Add children's names when appropriate. Read aloud each question in turn, and ask for answers. Through follow-up questions, explore *why* students came up with their answers. When several answers are given to an interpretive question, ask other children if they agree or disagree with what they have heard. Try to foster an exchange of opinion and to develop a few strong answers.

As in regular Shared Inquiry discussion, you will want to encourage students to give reasons for their answers by referring to the text. Children need not be able to read a passage in order to substantiate their opinions—recalling a line or a part of the text and paraphrasing it for the group is perfectly acceptable. If children are unable at first to supply textual evidence themselves, model the practice by reading aloud a passage that you think contains textual evidence for their opinions. Then ask children to explain how the passage supports their answers. In this way, students will become aware that their opinions should be based on the text, and as their reading skills develop, so will their ability to find and cite evidence on their own.

After a number of responses have been given to a question, ask children whether they have all heard an answer that satisfies them. If some students indicate that they are not yet satisfied, have them contribute additional answers at this time. Then proceed to the next question. Conclude discussion by reiterating that all the opinions offered helped everyone understand the story or poem better.

Textual analysis replaces Sharing Questions Discussion as the interpretive discussion activity in some units. Textual analysis is a way for students to look closely at and interpret rich passages in a story or poem. When children focus on a limited portion of the text in this way, they develop respect for the author's words and a sensitivity to their precise meanings. In the Read-Aloud program, textual analysis is also used to help students refresh their memories and clarify their ideas, in preparation for dramatizations or interpretive drawing assignments.

Conduct a textual analysis by reading the poem or passage to the class, pausing to ask questions about lines or words that you think are worth exploring. Ask questions about what a character is thinking, about the significance of details, or about the meaning of particular phrases. Refer to the textual analysis questions printed in the margin of your text for examples of the kinds of questions to ask.

As you go through a passage, give children time to share answers and to think of their own questions if they can. Although some of your questions will have factual answers that the group can readily supply, many of your questions will be interpretive. Pursue interpretive questions with follow-up questions, just as you would in discussion.

M Y   F A V O R I T E   W O R D S

AN OPTIONAL ACTIVITY

At the end of each volume, pages are set aside for children to write down their "favorite words"—any words in the selections that they found especially memorable. Pinpointing and copying favorite words is a good way for children to increase their sight vocabularies.

Explain to your class that their favorite words can be new or unfamiliar, but they don't have to be. They can be any words or combinations of words that students find intriguing, unusual, or especially effective—for example, a word that is simply fun to say, or one that conveys a vivid picture.

If you plan to do a "My Favorite Words" activity, alert students before the second in-class reading. Students may underline their favorite words in the text during this second reading. After the reading, ask students for their favorite words, then write them on the board and briefly discuss the meaning of each. If appropriate, help the class consider any special features of the word that enrich its meaning, such as how it sounds or what associations it has.

A class collection of favorite words could also be kept on a special, decorated Read-Aloud bulletin board, which would enable children to share and discuss their words outside of Read-Aloud time. Encourage children to keep a record of their favorite words from each selection by having them copy their words on the "My Favorite Words" page at the end of each Read-Aloud volume. Children might also want to add brief definitions on the "My Favorite Words" page. If so, they can either write a definition or draw one as an art note.

"My Favorite Words" is also a pleasant activity for children to work on at home. For example, the adult partner could help the child locate and underline favorite words during the at-home reading. The adult might also help the child record words on the "My Favorite Words" page at the end of the session.

Additional suggestions for using favorite words include asking students to select a word (or words) from their "My Favorite Words" page and write a story or poem in which that word appears. Students might also choose a favorite word to work into a drawing. For example, children could:

Illustrate the word. Ask children to draw a picture or series of small pictures that show the word's meaning or the associations it has for the child. For example, for the word "splendor" a student might depict rays surrounding the word, or draw small pictures of such objects as a star, a sun, a rainbow, or a jewel.

Make a concrete poem. Tell children that they can use the word itself (along with other words if they like) to make a picture or design. Show some examples of shaped verse, such as poems in the shape of a Christmas tree or heart, to help them get started. Encourage children to choose a shape or pattern that is appropriate to the word.

Write a hieroglyphic story or sentence. Ask children to incorporate their favorite word in a sentence or story otherwise written in pictures. Have them share and "read" each other's stories.

THE ART ACTIVITIES

Creating original art based on a reading selection is a natural and appealing way for children to connect with literature. Whenever children are asked to visualize a scene or a character through drawing, they are learning to translate the language of literature into concrete pictures. Words on a page are no longer abstractions, but become real to the child as he or she draws.

The process of visualizing some aspect of a literary work is a form of interpretation. To draw a picture of a character, for example, is to express an interpretation of that character's personality. Before drawing the Pied Piper, children are given the opportunity to consider various words that might be used to describe him, such as "greedy," "fair," "scary," and "smart." They then choose those words (including any of their own) that they think best fit the Piper's character. In other instances, such as in the unit on "Chestnut Pudding," children are asked to illustrate their favorite scene. Even this simple activity contributes to the interpretive process. For in choosing a scene to depict, children not only visualize characters and setting, but also express which part of the story they find most meaningful.

All of the art assignments in the Read-Aloud program are interpretive in the sense that they require the child to think about the text and to formulate a response or an opinion. Because most of the artwork is done in the student books, each child is, in effect, making a permanent record of his or her own unique vision of the story or poem. To ensure that the interpretive element is preserved in all of the art activities, the professional illustrations in the books are carefully chosen so as not to interfere with or influence the drawings the children are asked to do. The professional drawings are rendered in black and white rather than color so that the main visual emphasis remains on the children's own artwork.

In the Read-Aloud program, the drawing assignments are designed to maximize interpretive potential. For instance, the actual drawing may be preceded by a brief class discussion of the assignment. Having children write or dictate captions for their pictures is another way to extend their interpretive thinking. Incomplete captions are included on some of the drawing pages, and help to bring the particular interpretive issue into focus. For example, the incomplete caption "The boy loves the mermaid because . . ." directs students to look into the "whys" behind the events in "The Mermaid Who Lost Her Comb," and to pinpoint what is for them the most significant reason.

Especially important for promoting the concept of different, individual interpretations is the "share and compare" component of the art activities. These opportunities to share artwork can become miniature interpretive discussions in which children informally articulate their ideas and hear others' comments and insights. Depending on your preference and the arrangement of your classroom, you may try any of several ways of helping children share their art. If your children sit in small groups at tables, encourage them to explain their pictures to you and to other students in their group, as you circulate during the drawing sessions. You may also have children take turns holding up their pictures before the whole class, talking about their work, and answering questions. If you have children do additional, related art projects, such as bringing in pieces of "found art" relevant to the theme of the week, these projects can be displayed in the room on a Read-Aloud bulletin board, where children can point out and discuss their contributions with other class members.

Art assignments in the Read-Aloud program are specifically tailored to each selection and represent several different types of activities. These activities include frontispieces, partially-completed drawings, drawing an answer to an interpretive or evaluative question, "mood drawings," art notes, and personal-response drawings.

Frontispieces give children an opportunity to record their early reactions to and impressions of a story. Assignments for frontispieces vary, but all are things children would be eager to do immediately after hearing the selection. Moreover, these are assignments that children can do without the interpretive insights they will acquire during subsequent readings and discussion. For example, children might be invited to work with their initial understanding of a character in an imaginative way, such as drawing what they think Zlateh in "Zlateh the Goat" would look like if she were a person. Or, children may be asked to interpret a striking central image in the story, such as drawing their interpretation of the witch's bread house in "Hansel and Gretel."

Partially-completed drawings give children the opportunity to concentrate on an interpretive issue, while providing them with a helpful context and visual stimulus. For example, in the unit on "The Pied Piper," the professional drawing of the medieval town gives children information they need in order to visualize the setting of the story, but leaves them free to express their own interpretation of the rats that overran the town of Franchville.

Drawing an answer to an interpretive or evaluative question enables all children, whatever their level of language skill, to communicate their thinking about the selection. In the unit on "The Mermaid Who Lost Her Comb," the interpretive question "Why is Haskeir the perfect home for the young man and the mermaid?" requires students to stretch their understanding of both main characters when they create their drawing. Two of the drawings for the "Hansel and Gretel" unit express each student's considered opinion regarding the bravest thing Hansel did and the bravest thing Gretel did in the story.

Mood drawings increase the range of artistic expression by allowing children to use color, pattern, and personal symbolism, rather than a representational approach, to convey an interpretation of the mood or feeling of something that happens in the story or poem. Mood drawings help children both explore their more subjective responses to the text and empathize with the characters or situations. For instance, after reading

"Zlateh the Goat," students are asked to depict the feelings they might have if, like Aaron, they were caught in a blizzard, and the feelings they might have after the storm was over. Freed from concern about producing an accurate picture of something, students can experiment with more imaginative ways of conveying such possible responses as "fear," "relief," or "joy."

Art notes are smaller drawings or sketches that allow students to follow a pattern in the text and to comment briefly on it at several points. These sketches are the artistic equivalent of the written notes that older children make in the Junior Great Books program. Since art notes are done as a series, they represent a slight departure from the more usual type of illustration. Therefore, you may want to help students get started by explaining at the outset of the activity how many art notes will be drawn, where they belong, and how they are connected. For example, the two art notes children make on "The Quangle Wangle's Hat" give them a chance to visualize some of the creatures named in two different stanzas of the poem. To help children understand that the art note is intended to be only a quick sketch and not an elaborate work of art, you might suggest that they do their notes in pencil (to be colored later, if desired).

Personal-response drawings invite students to use personal experience or imaginings to create a work of art that in some way parallels or extends the text just read. For example, after reading the poem "The Dumb Soldier," in which the speaker imagines being as tiny as a toy soldier and experiencing the mysterious world in the grass, students are asked to draw a picture of a place *they* would like to visit if they had no human limitations.

If time permits, you may want children to do additional drawings based on the selections, or related art projects using different media, such as collages, murals, or clay figures. For example, one suggestion would be to make a large decorated hat for "The Quangle Wangle's Hat." Further art activity can be introduced into the program by asking children to illustrate their writing assignments or by adopting some of the suggestions discussed in the "My Favorite Words" section.

DRAMATIZATION

Most children love acting out a story. It is a way for them to recapture the pleasure of the story and to share imaginatively in the adventures of the characters. Children's pretending also plays a special part in learning. Children often act out a new experience or idea in order to make it their own, so they can understand and use it. Dramatizations in the Read-Aloud program are designed to build on both aspects of pretending—joyful play and a way of thinking over something new.

Early in a unit, dramatizations can help children grasp a story or poem. Acting out unfamiliar situations makes them seem more concrete, and incidents in a long or complicated plot become more connected. A dramatization is more than a plot review, however; it also helps children empathize with characters and consider their motives. As children dramatize key events in the boy's quest for chestnuts in "Chestnut Pudding," for example, they are able to participate more fully in the boy's adventure and consider why he is so successful.

Later in a unit, dramatization also serves as a way for children to put together their ideas about a story to build a comprehensive interpretation. When discussing G.B.'s questions or participating in Sharing Questions Discussion, children focus on separate issues—a single incident or a single character's action—that might be interpreted several ways. When acting out a story, a child can explore different possible meanings and make a choice of the one that seems best. Moreover, while acting, a child will keep trying to realize the meanings of details in such a way that the story as a whole will hang together. By acting out several key scenes in "Mother of the Waters," for instance, children can portray their understanding of why the old woman tests the two girls, as well as show what they think each girl reveals about herself.

Through such dramatizations, children are able to express a genuine interpretation of the story. They can experience, in an enjoyable way, the same process of thought by which an accomplished reader considers the possible meanings of parts of a story and reflects on the story as a whole. This experience is reinforced if children turn to a complementary way of expressing their interpretive insights, such as drawing, discussion, or writing.

For all dramatizations, then, the aim is to let children make their own decisions about character interpretation, while focusing strongly on the story itself. Your role is to set up a framework in which children can work together easily, concentrating on the story they all have heard (rather than making up new versions or improvising on personal experiences). When possible, ask questions or even conduct a textual analysis to help students become more aware of the interpretations they are making when they act.

If your class has had little experience with dramatization, you will want to set up an acting project in a fairly simple way. For example, for the poem "The Quangle Wangle's Hat," children might pretend to be their imaginary animals and together act out the dance on the Quangle Wangle's hat. Of course, as a simplification of any dramatic activity, you can always have students act out parts of a story or an entire poem as a group.

A somewhat more sophisticated way of handling dramatization is to assign a role to every child. In addition to portraying minor characters, children can play trees or wild animals of the forest, huts and gingerbread houses, and so forth, setting the scene by acting scary, friendly, welcoming, or indifferent. Designate a stage—probably the center of the room—and place groups of actors at different stations, so they can be ready together to go "on stage." Read the story aloud while children act, or read transitional parts while children fill in dialogue and action. Less experienced actors might find it too hard to act out only selected scenes in a story; you will save time in the long run by letting them cover the whole story. Try to keep the action from dragging or being interrupted. As students gain confidence, encourage them to prompt each other, to suggest details, and to direct themselves.

When a class is more experienced with dramatization, you can help them reflect more on the story while they act. Pause after especially interesting scenes to ask children how characters felt or why they acted as they did. You can also divide a more experienced class into two groups and hold back-to-back dramatizations, so that children may see and discuss differences in interpretations.

T H E   W R I T I N G   A C T I V I T I E S

Whether they write independently or "write" orally in a group, all beginning readers can benefit from composing original work. Writing extends the process of finding meaning in literature, and helps children improve their sight vocabularies. Writing about a story or poem not only stimulates interpretive thinking, it endows those thoughts with a special importance. As an author, a child gains a sense of confidence in approaching any language-related work and develops a new way of appreciating literature.

The writing activities in the Read-Aloud program are designed to accommodate all children, whatever their inclinations or abilities. Like the art activities, the writing activities are done in the children's own books, enabling students to keep a permanent record of their thoughts about each selection.

"My Questions" are written or dictated by children after the second reading, and allow students to capture their initial curiosity about the selection. "My Questions" are first shared with the parent at the conclusion of the at-home session. They are later shared with classmates and teacher through the Sharing Questions bulletin board. It is a great source of pride for students to see their questions displayed and to hear them referred to during class discussion. If you like, the "My Question" pages can be stapled or pasted back into students' books when the unit is completed.

Captions for drawings are brief, manageable compositions that children can either dictate or write. Suitable at any stage of work on a particular text, captions give students an opportunity to clarify the interpretive content of a drawing by providing an explanation of the picture or answering a question. Caption lines on the drawing pages often include the first few words, to focus the interpretive issue and to act as a "starter" for children's writing.

Writing an answer to a question or a reason to back up an answer gives students an opportunity to reflect on and apply their more developed understanding of the text. For example, at the conclusion of work on "Mother of the Waters," children write a reason to support their "yes" or "no" answer to the evaluative question "Do you like the way the Mother of the Waters treats the girls?"

Creative-writing assignments are offered in Session 3 or Session 4 of many units and usually take the form of a group project, such as a collaborative poem or paragraph. Coming late in the week's schedule of activities, the creative-writing assignments are intended to give students an opportunity to consolidate some of their previous interpretive work in the unit and to think further about some aspect of the selection. For instance, in the final activity for "The Mermaid Who Lost Her Comb," children "make a comb" by writing a comb-shaped poem that expresses what they think the boy wants to tell the mermaid. The final creative project for "The Pied Piper" asks students to work with the music of the story's language and to think about the way the Piper's songs appeal to different audiences by composing their own "Song of the Rats."

Group writing projects—with children making oral contributions as you record them on a chalkboard or chart paper—are a fun way to engage in creative writing. The whole class shares responsibility for the finished product, and children's ideas can flow freely since students themselves do not have to be concerned about the mechanics of writing.

Begin a group writing activity by explaining the object of the assignment and how you will proceed. For example, you might collect ideas from the whole class first and refine them later, or you may have each student contribute one line. If the poem has a pattern of lines or some "starters" (first lines or beginnings of lines) provided in the student books, it is helpful to copy these on the board. To help students get ideas, use questions such as those suggested in the directions for specific assignments and add others of your own. Also use questions to coax out details and more expressive language.

Sample poems are often provided to clarify directions and to assist you in thinking of questions you might ask to elicit ideas and lines from your students. The samples are not meant to be read or copied by the class. The poem structures provided are intended to give children a helpful framework for their ideas. These structures can, of course, be made shorter or longer to accomodate your class's work. Assure children that their poems need not have rhyme or a specific rhythm unless they wish, but do try to help them make their lines vivid and descriptive.

Writing activities in the Read-Aloud program are meant to be flexible in application, so that all students, regardless of their level of skill, can participate in the writing process and enjoy the satisfaction of seeing a written product they have helped create. In addition to whole-class oral composition with the teacher as recorder, you might try having children work in small groups with one child as the designated writer. Or, have children write their own poems individually, perhaps after a class discussion to help them get started. In some cases, you might find it helpful to describe the assignment the day before you plan to do it in class, and let children think about, or write out, their contributions at home before pooling them in a group writing activity. As a general rule, you may want to do mostly oral group composition in the first semester, moving on to introduce more small-group or individual versions of the projects in the second semester or with more able writers.

Entering group compositions in the students' books can also be adapted to suit your class's requirements. If your students find copying from the board laborious, you might consider providing copies of the completed projects for them to staple or paste onto the appropriate pages in their books. More experienced writers can do their own transcribing of favorite lines—or even the whole composition—from the board.

If you wish, you can easily expand the writing component of the Read-Aloud program. Students can be asked to provide captions for drawings that do not already require them, or caption ideas might be enlarged into paragraphs or stories to accompany the art assignments. Other possibilities include having students write stories or poems incorporating one or more words from their "My Favorite Words" lists, or asking them to write answers to their own "My Questions" or the interpretive questions you lead in discussion.

T H E   P O E T R Y   U N I T S

One unit of each volume in the Pegasus Series consists of a group of three poems that are linked by a common theme, but are not interdependent. The structure of the poetry units is similar to that of the story units. The first poem, which is the longest or most substantial of the three, is dealt with in the first two class sessions and in the intervening at-home session. The second and third poems receive one class session apiece. However, the modular nature of the poetry units allows for flexibility in scheduling. For example, you may sometimes find it more convenient to do two poems instead of all three or to add an extra session during the week.

Aside from offering variety, working with poetry gives children an opportunity to enjoy literature that places a special emphasis on the pleasures of language—the delightful sounds of words and the compelling rhythms of lines. We stress these features by including plenty of activities that allow children to recite and act out or dance to poems. The rhymes, rhythms, and sound effects of verse enable even inexperienced readers and nonreaders to memorize and repeat selections, while the short lines and stanza breaks make it easy for children who have some reading skills to follow along for themselves. Reading poetry fosters appreciation of language for its own sake and helps stimulate children's willingness to experiment with language in their own writing. The poetry units also offer an excellent opportunity to make use of the optional "My Favorite Words" activity.

The poems, like the stories in the Read-Aloud program, are chosen for their ability to support interpretive activities, including discussion of interpretive or evaluative questions, drawing, dramatization, and group or individual writing. In some cases, the activities include a preliminary question for children to think about as they listen to the poem being read aloud. These questions prepare children to listen actively and move smoothly into discussion. Since the poems are relatively short, they can be read several times in a session. Thus, children are able to experience a feeling of real familiarity and comfort with the poem, which can translate into improved focus and concentration.

Because sound is such a vital part of poetry's appeal, you will probably want to practice reading a poem aloud a couple of times before presenting it in class. When reading aloud, let the poem's rhythm carry you, but don't change natural pronunciation to fit a set beat and don't *over*stress the accented syllables. Poets often vary even a pronounced rhythm to avoid monotony, and a metrical pattern is usually sufficiently apparent if you read in a normal tone of voice. Observe punctuation as you would with prose: if there is no punctuation at the end of a line, read right into the next line, and pause longer when a line ends with a period than when it ends with a comma. When beginning your first poetry unit, you may want to prepare children by offering a very brief introduction to the form. It should be sufficient to explain a few basic terms, such as "line" and "stanza," and to alert them to some of the main differences between poetry and prose. Before reading any particular poem, you may wish to mention some salient feature of that selection, such as the presence or absence of rhyme or the use of an unusual rhythm.

INVOLVING PARENTS

Adult partners for the at-home portion of the Read-Aloud program fill a vital role. Confidence in and commitment to reading grow when children experience a link between the worlds of home and school. Not only does learning become easier when parents and other adults actively participate in children's efforts to understand the written word, but students also absorb the important message that reading is worthwhile.

When you describe the at-home session to parents and guardians, you will want to communicate to them their special role as reader and as a relaxed, interested listener. When asking G.B.'s questions, the adult partner or parent should keep in mind that there are no single right answers, that considering these questions is just the beginning of the child's work with the story, and that answers shouldn't be considered final. Above all, the at-home session should be fun—a cozy reading time when children and adults can share some good talk.

Appendix B provides two sample letters to send home when you initiate your Read-Aloud program. The first letter explains what the Read-Aloud program is and alerts parents and guardians to their role as adult partner in the at-home session. The second letter provides a more detailed explanation of the adult partner's responsibilities. Another very effective means of cultivating active participation is to introduce the program, by means of a short talk or visual display, at an open house or at a PTA meeting. (See Appendix C for a sample presentation highlighting the benefits of the Read-Aloud program and describing parents' at-home role.)

Recruiting volunteers to assist with the Read-Aloud program in the classroom is another way to involve parents, older students, or community members. You could ask volunteers to prepare Read-Aloud bulletin boards, to help students write captions during the art activities, or to assist you in other ways. Some programs train volunteers to lead discussions. In kindergarten and first grade, this works best when teachers are also involved. For more information on training for either teachers or volunteers, visit www.greatbooks.org and click on Professional Development.

CHESTNUT PUDDING

IROQUOIS FOLKTALE
AS TOLD BY
JOHN BIERHORST

SESSION I

This session consists of an introduction and first reading of the story, followed by a brief sharing of questions and comments, and an art activity in which children draw their favorite part of the story.

AT-HOME WORK

During this second reading of the story, the adult partner encourages the child to join in saying the underlined words and phrases, and pauses to discuss G.B.'s three questions. When called for, children respond to these questions by circling their answer or by underlining parts of the story.

After reading, the adult writes the child's own question about the story into the book in preparation for the Sharing Questions Discussion (Session 3).

SESSION 2

During this reading of the story, you will collect students' responses to G.B.'s questions and lead a discussion of them. You will also pause to have students dramatize parts of the boy's adventure.

SESSION 3

This session consists of a Sharing Questions Discussion and an art activity to help children visualize the key incident in the story—when the boy enters the mole's body in order to complete his quest.

SESSION 4

This session consists of a choral activity in which the class chants the boy's song to the witches, and a group creative-writing activity in which children write a chant that the boy could sing as he scatters the chestnuts.

SESSION 1

INTRODUCTION

Begin the session by telling children that the story they are going to hear is about a Native American boy who lived long ago with his grandmother in a very different kind of home. Show students the illustration of the boy's house (page 10), drawing attention to its smoke hole.

FIRST READING AND SHARING OF RESPONSES

Ask students to listen as you read the story aloud. To make sure the class knows what a mole looks like, point out the illustration at the end of the story.

After the reading, allow a few moments to clear up unfamiliar vocabulary and to let students ask questions and share their initial reactions to the story. Encourage children to offer their opinions about which parts of the story they especially liked and why, in preparation for the art activity.

ART ACTIVITY

Have children create the frontispiece by drawing their favorite part of the story. As children work, circulate among them and help them write captions in the space provided. Allow time for students to share and compare their illustrations.

SESSION 2

POSTING "MY QUESTIONS"

Have students cut out the questions they wrote at home and pin them on the Sharing Questions bulletin board. Children who have not had an at-home reading can dictate their questions to you at this time. Encourage children to look at the Sharing Questions bulletin board during the week, to point out their own questions and to ask about those of their classmates.

READING AND REVIEW OF G.B.'S QUESTIONS

Read the story aloud, encouraging children to follow along in their books. Pause to collect students' responses to G.B.'s questions (pages 9, 16, and 20). Encourage them to give reasons for their answers, and help them elaborate on their responses by asking follow-up questions such as those printed in the margin of your text.

DRAMATIZATION

Between discussion of G.B.'s first and second questions, have students dramatize key events in the boy's quest—his encounters with the gorge, the rattlesnakes, and the panthers (pages 14-15). Pause during your reading to have different children act out the three scenes in turn.

SESSION 3

SHARING QUESTIONS DISCUSSION

Prepare for discussion as usual, deciding on the five or six interpretive questions you intend to ask the class. Note which of the children's questions are similar to those you plan to lead and try to include three or four of their questions in your final list. When you write your questions on the board, include children's names as appropriate.

Suggested Interpretive Questions

Why does the grandmother keep her chestnut pudding a secret?

Why isn't the boy afraid to try his grandmother's magic?

Why does the boy succeed in getting the chestnuts, after he foolishly wasted those his grandmother had?

Why doesn't the boy tell his grandmother how he defeated the witches and got the chestnuts?

ART ACTIVITY

Ask children to turn to the page captioned "The Boy in the Mole's Body." Briefly remind them of the episode in which the boy enters the mole's body and have them recall some of the reasons they gave for why the boy chose a mole to be his helper. Then ask them to draw a picture showing the boy inside the mole. To help students consider what this might have been like for the boy, ask them such questions as *What would it feel like to be inside a mole's body? Would you feel like a mole, or like yourself?*

SESSION 4

CHORAL ACTIVITY

Have children turn to the boy's song to the witches on page 19, and remind them of what is happening in the story. Explain that a chant is like a magic command—the boy's chant told the witches what they had to do. Read the song through once or twice, with the children repeating it after you; ask them to try to make it sound magic. Then ask one child to beat out a rhythm on the desk, while the class repeats the song to that rhythm. Try two or three different versions, with different children as drummers.

SESSION 4 (continued)

GROUP CREATIVE WRITING

Tell the class that together they will now write a chant that the boy could sing as he scatters the chestnuts. To help generate ideas, read aloud the paragraph on page 21 beginning, "So be it," and ending, "and many were planted." Then ask children such questions as *Why is this a wonderful thing? What will happen as a result of scattering the chestnuts? How will things be different for the people of the boy's tribe from the way they were at the beginning of the story?*

Write on the board the chant's title, "The Chestnut-Scattering Chant," and the last line, "What a wonderful thing this is!" Ask children to suggest lines that the grandmother and the boy could chant to the chestnuts while they scatter them—what would they tell the chestnuts to do?

As children offer suggestions, help them make their lines concrete in meaning and interesting in sound. Write completed lines on the board. When the chant is finished, read it back to the class and ask them to repeat it after you. Make copies for students to paste in their books on the page provided, or have them copy the chant themselves.

Here is an example of a chant that a class might compose:

The Chestnut-Scattering Chant

Come now, you chestnuts!
Wake up and grow
wake up and grow
freed from the seven sisters
   and your eagle guard;
   make us food forever
     forever.
What a wonderful thing this is!

CHESTNUT PUDDING

IROQUOIS FOLKTALE

In a small lodge deep in the woods an old woman lived with her grandson. Every day she would cook food for the little boy, but she herself would never eat.

One evening, when the fire was hot and potatoes and moss were simmering, the boy asked his grandmother to sit down and have supper with him. "I will eat some other time," she said. "This food is for you alone."

The boy finished, then said, "Oh, grandmother, I am sleepy. I have to lie down now and get some rest," and with these words he wrapped himself in an old piece of skin and began to snore as if he were sound asleep.

But the skin had a tiny hole in it, and through the hole the boy was watching to see what his grandmother would do.

When the old woman was satisfied
that her grandson was sleeping, she
took out a bark case from under her bed
and carefully opened it. Inside were
a tiny kettle, a red-willow wand, and a
piece of food. Holding the food in
her hand, she scraped off a few crumbs
into the kettle and added water.

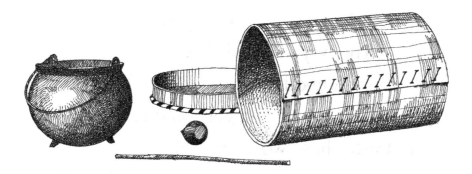

When it began to boil, she tapped
the kettle gently with the wand and
sang the words, "**Now, my kettle, I want
you to grow.**" As she sang, the kettle
became large and filled up with pudding.

She ate the pudding quickly, and as soon as she was finished, she washed the kettle, shook it to make it small again, then put everything back in the hiding place under her bed.

The next day, while the grandmother was out getting firewood, the boy searched under her bed until he found the things he had seen her use the night before. The tiny piece of food seemed hardly enough for one portion, so he scraped all of it into the kettle and began to tap with the wand.

The kettle became enormous. It grew so large the boy had to use a paddle to stir the pudding. As it boiled, making the sound **bub bub bub bub bub**, it began to overflow and fill the room around the fire.

Is the boy acting babyish or grown-up when he tries out his grandmother's magic?
(Circle your answer.)

BABYISH

GROWN-UP

Is the boy mad at his grandmother for keeping her magic a secret?

Why doesn't he worry that he's using up all his grandmother's food?

By eating her food, do you think he is trying to be like his grandmother?

The boy jumped onto the bed
and kept stirring. Then he climbed to the
rafters and finally to the roof. Running
around the smoke hole, he kept on
stirring the pudding, which now filled
the entire lodge.

Suddenly he saw his grandmother
hurrying out of the woods. Looking
up, she could see her grandson running
in circles on the roof. When she
reached the door of the lodge, she saw
the bark flaps bulging and the pudding
already starting to spill out.

Immediately she blew on the
pudding, and it shrank back. She blew
harder. It shrank more, and she kept on
blowing until it was all gone. Then
she called to her grandson, "Come, now,
get down from there."

Her voice was sad. As the boy
crawled off the roof, she said to him,
"You have used up all my food. There
is nothing else I can eat. That little
piece would have lasted me many years."

Wrapping herself in a skin robe,
she added, "I may as well lie down
right here. Hunger will finish me off."
Having said this, she lay on the ground
and covered herself up completely.

"Grandmother," cried the boy,
"what is the name of this food?"

"It is called chestnut," she said,
speaking through the robe.

"And where does it grow?"

"It is of no use for me to tell
you. How could you ever get to it? You
are only a little boy." Her voice was
muffled. But she continued, saying, "The
chestnut tree is owned by seven sisters,
who are witches, and the path to their
lodge is guarded by living things
that would attack you."

"And where is the path?"

"Toward the rising sun."

Then the boy left on a swift run.
All day he raced, until the sun was
low in the west and he saw as he passed
through a clearing that the woods'
edges were hidden in dew clouds.
There he built a fire and camped for
the night.

Standing close to the fire and
holding a pinch of tobacco he had taken
from his pouch, he said, "Come, now,
listen to me, you, all kinds of animals
and you, too, who have formed and made
my life." With these words he threw
the tobacco into the fire, then cried out,
"Now, listen. The smoke is rising.
I ask you to help me."

The next morning he started
early, hurrying on toward the east. It
wasn't long before he came to a steep
gorge, too steep to climb into and
too wide to jump across. Then he talked
to the gorge: "Earth, why are you
broken? This is unheard of. **I won't allow
it. Close up!**" And the earth closed
with a loud snap.

He kept on until he came to
two giant rattlesnakes standing guard
over the path. They opened their
jaws and began to rattle. But the boy
talked to them: "Rattlesnakes, go
away. **Get out of my path. Be ashamed!**"

14

Frightened, the rattlesnakes closed their jaws and hurried off into the woods.

The boy ran on. Suddenly two panthers appeared, one on each side of the path. He ran straight toward them. "Panthers," he said, **"you are free to go. Get out of my way!"**

Surprised by the boy's words, the panthers drew back and let him pass.

He ran on, until at last the trees began to thin out and he could see a lodge in the distance at the far side of a clearing. Next to the lodge stood the chestnut tree, guarded by an eagle perched at the top.

Why does the boy choose a mole to be his helper? (Underline one or two things on this page that help you answer this question.)

Why can the tiny mole get past the eagle?

Why does the boy want to move underground? Why does he want to move quickly?

Knowing that he would have to be careful, the boy called for a mole, saying, "Now, my friend, I want you to come to me. Come to me, you mole." In a short time the leaves began to rustle at his feet, and a mole appeared, asking, "What do you want?"

The boy replied, "My grandmother is in trouble. I scraped away her last chestnut. Now you must help me get her some more. Let me fit inside your body. Take me underground to that tree in the far corner of the clearing, and don't let the eagle hear us."

When the boy had entered the mole's body, it made its way quickly to the roots of the tree. Then it pushed its nose and mouth up through the dry leaves, and the boy stuck his ear out of the mole's mouth to listen for sounds from the lodge.

16

The Boy in the Mole's Body

Hearing nothing, he jumped to his
full size, shook a bag from his pouch,
and filled it with chestnuts. He had turned
to go and was just running off when
the eagle heard him and gave a scream.

At once the seven sisters came
out of their lodge, waving their war clubs,
shouting, "Someone has stolen our
chestnuts. Catch him!"

The boy ran as fast as he could,
but the witches kept coming nearer. He
could hear their footsteps close behind
him. Suddenly he turned around and
began to beat on the bag of chestnuts
as though it were a drum. "Now you
will dance," he cried. And he sang:

> **to the upper side**
> **of the sky**
> **to the upper side**
> **of the sky**
> **and never return**
> **and never return**

Why is the boy's magic stronger than the witches' magic?

Why does the boy beat on the bag of chestnuts as though it were a drum?

Why does the boy make the witches dance to the upper sky, never to return?

Why is the boy more entitled to the chestnuts than the witches?

He kept on drumming as the sisters rose into the air, half as high as the tallest trees, and all the while they were dancing. They rose still higher and soon disappeared in the sky.

The boy ran on, not stopping until the sun went under the hills and the black night came. Again he made camp, and in the morning he continued on his way, arriving at his grandmother's in time to hear her say, "Oh, grandson, you have come, and I am still alive." The boy rushed into the lodge, letting the bag of chestnuts fall—with the sound **pumh**! It was very heavy.

"Grandson, tell me," cried the
old woman, "how did you ever do it?"

"I, of course, know how I did it,
but I will tell you only this: that I got
rid of all those witches."

"So be it," she said. "What a wonderful
thing this is." Then they scattered handfuls
of chestnuts, and many were planted.

From that time on, the grandmother
always had enough to eat, and
somewhere, deep in the woods, they
say, she is still making chestnut puddings.

The Chestnut-Scattering Chant

_____

_____

_____

_____

_____

_____

_____

What a wonderful thing this is!

My Question

_____

_____

_____

Name _____

THE PIED PIPER

ENGLISH FOLKTALE

AS TOLD BY

JOSEPH JACOBS

♫

OVERVIEW

SESSION 1

This session consists of an introduction and first reading of the story, followed by a brief sharing of questions and comments, and an art activity in which children draw the rats of Franchville.

AT-HOME WORK

During this second reading, the adult partner pauses to discuss G.B.'s three questions. Children respond to these questions by circling either "yes" or "no."

After reading, the adult writes the child's own question about the story into the book in preparation for the Sharing Questions Discussion (Session 4).

SESSION 2

During this reading of the story, you will collect students' responses to G.B.'s questions and lead a discussion of them. The session concludes with an art activity in which students draw what they think the children of Franchville heard in the Piper's song.

SESSION 3

This session consists of a vocabulary activity that focuses on words that might be used to describe the Piper, and an art activity in which students draw their interpretation of the Pied Piper.

SESSION 4

This session consists of a Sharing Questions Discussion and a group creative-writing activity in which students make up their own "Song of the Rats."

SESSION 1

INTRODUCTION

Begin the session by telling your class that the story takes place in England a long time ago. Explain the title by defining "pied" and "Pied Piper," using the definitions given in the margin of your text.

FIRST READING AND SHARING OF RESPONSES

Ask children to listen as you read the story aloud. After the reading, allow a few moments to clear up unfamiliar vocabulary and to let students ask questions and share their initial reactions to the story. Because the story contains a rather high proportion of unusual words, it would be advisable to downplay questions about vocabulary. Most of the words can be sufficiently understood from context and are best appreciated as part of the distinctive overall style of the tale.

ART ACTIVITY

Have students turn to the frontispiece, captioned "The Rats of Franchville." Explain that the picture isn't finished; it shows the town of Franchville, but students need to complete the picture by drawing in the rats that lived there before the Pied Piper came along. Help children get ideas for their pictures by asking such questions as *Do you think the rats are scary? selfish? ugly? funny? When you think of the rats do you imagine them having a great jolly party, or do you think of them threatening the people?*

Allow time for students to share and compare their illustrations.

SESSION 2

POSTING "MY QUESTIONS"

Have students cut out the questions they wrote at home and pin them on the Sharing Questions bulletin board. Children who have not had an at-home reading can dictate their questions to you at this time. Encourage children to look at the Sharing Questions bulletin board during the week, to point out their own questions and to ask about those of their classmates.

READING AND REVIEW OF G.B.'S QUESTIONS

Read the story aloud, encouraging children to follow along in their books. Pause to collect students' responses to G.B.'s questions (pages 32, 34, and 37). Help students think further about their reasons for their answers by asking additional questions such as those given in the margin of your text.

SESSION 2 (continued)

ART ACTIVITY

Have students turn to the page at the end of the story captioned "The children are imagining...." Remind students that the Piper is able to lead the children of Franchville away by playing a song of "happy laughter and merry play." Read aloud the passage on page 35 beginning, "And as he paced down the streets the elders mocked," and ending on page 36, "forest full of old oaks and wide-spreading beeches." Tell students that they are going to draw what they think the children of Franchville hear in the Piper's song. Help them develop their ideas by asking such questions as *What sort of fun are the children imagining as they listen to the Piper's song? Where do they imagine that the Piper is leading them? What do they expect to find there?*

Encourage students to discuss their ideas as they draw. Circulate during the activity and help students write captions for their pictures. Allow time for children to share and compare their drawings.

SESSION 3

VOCABULARY ACTIVITY

Have students turn to the page at the end of the story captioned "The Pied Piper." Tell students that the words at the top of this page are words that different people might use to describe the Pied Piper. Write the words on the board one at a time and for each one ask, "Do you think the Pied Piper is _____?" Try to elicit a few different reasons, supported by the story, for both "yes" and "no" answers. Then have students circle the words that they think fit the Piper. Make clear that they might circle several different words, or all, or only one.

ART ACTIVITY

Tell students that now that they have thought about different words to describe the Pied Piper, they are going to draw a picture of him that shows what kind of person they think he is.

SESSION 4

SHARING QUESTIONS DISCUSSION

Prepare for discussion as usual, deciding on the five or six interpretive questions you intend to ask the class. Note which of the children's questions are similar to those you plan to lead and try to include three or four of their questions in your final list. When you write your questions on the board, include children's names as appropriate.

Suggested Interpretive Questions

Why does the Piper wear clothes of many colors?

Why aren't the townspeople grateful enough to pay the Piper what they had promised?

When the Pied Piper leads the children away, is he rescuing them or punishing the townspeople?

GROUP CREATIVE WRITING

Remind students that in the story the Pied Piper has a special kind of song for every audience. When he calls the children, he plays a tune that sounds like happy laughter and play. When he calls the rats, he plays a tune that sounds like rats. Tell students that the class is now going to make up its own "Song of the Rats."

Write on the board the title "Song of the Rats" and the beginning of the poem, "We are the rats!/Listen to the sound of our...."

Explain that the poem will describe what rats do and the sounds they make, and that you will write the lines students create on the board. Help the class get started by suggesting word patterns from the story that they could imitate or add to, such as "squeaking and shrieking" or "hurrying and scurrying." Some other patterns that you might try include:

pairs (pittering and pattering)
triplets (pawing and gnawing and clawing)
repeated words (scratch, scratch, scratch)
sound effects (eek, eek)

To make the poem more songlike, have students try to give each line a special sound and let them work with each pattern for a while before suggesting another. Encourage students to invent suitable words (for example, "scritching" to go with "scratching").

When the poem is finished, read it back to the class. Make copies for students to paste in their books on the page provided, or have them copy the poem themselves.

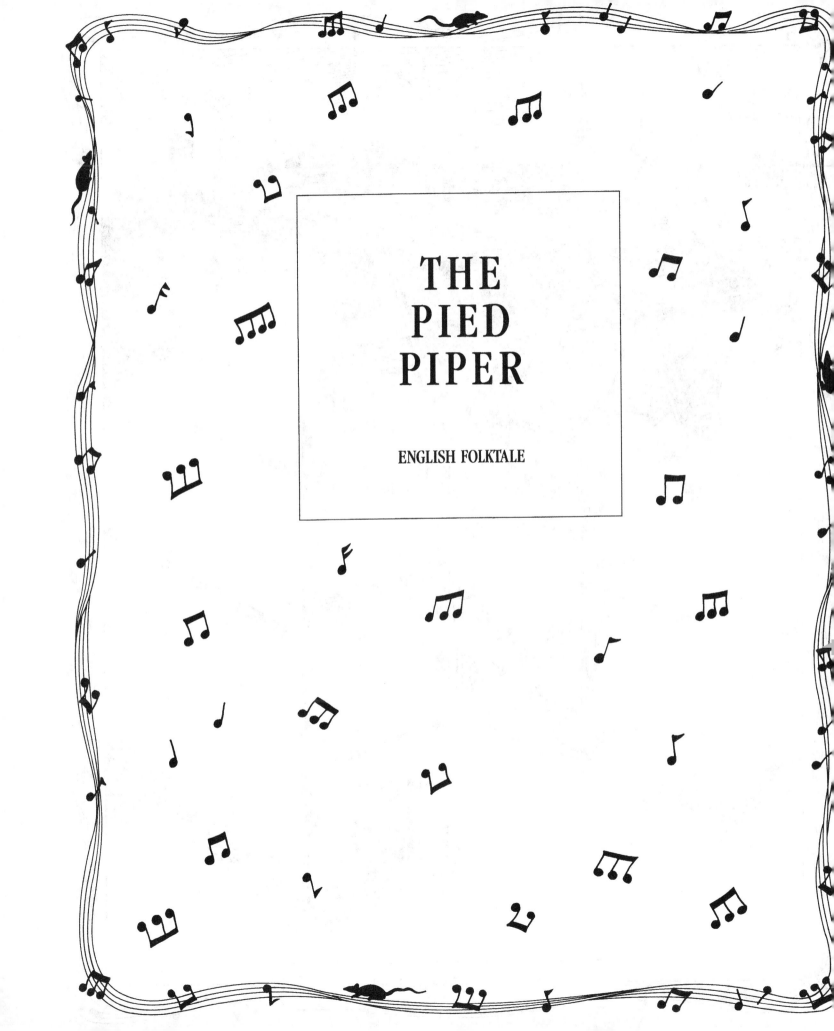

THE
PIED
PIPER

ENGLISH FOLKTALE

The Rats of Franchville

Newtown, or Franchville, as 'twas
called of old, is a sleepy little town,
as you all may know, upon the Solent
shore. Sleepy as it is now, it was
once noisy enough, and what made the
noise was—rats. The place was so infested
with them as to be scarce worth living
in. There wasn't a barn or a cornrick,
a storeroom or a cupboard, but they
ate their way into it. Not a cheese but they
gnawed it hollow, not a sugar puncheon
but they cleared out. Why the very
mead and beer in the barrels was
not safe from them. They'd gnaw
a hole in the top of the tun, and down
would go one master rat's tail, and
when he brought it up round would
crowd all the friends and cousins,
and each would have a suck at the tail.

pied: having patches or spots of many colors

Pied Piper: person who plays a flute or pipe and wears an outfit of many colors

Solent: the channel between England and the Isle of Wight

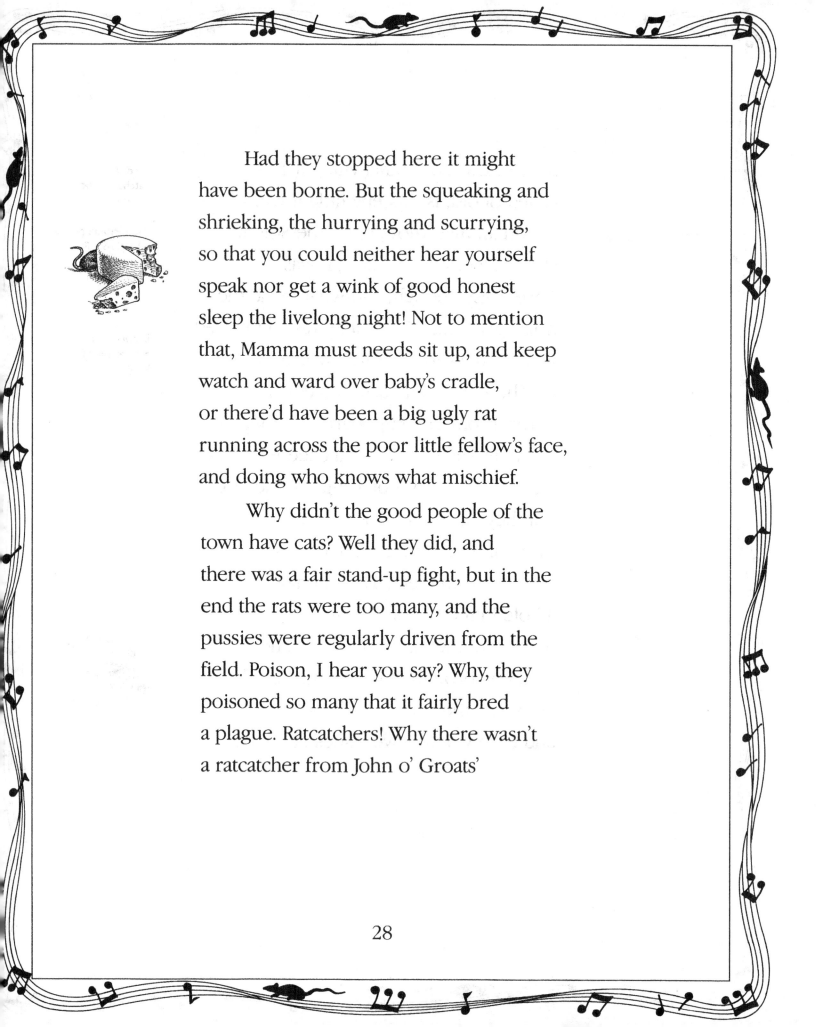

Had they stopped here it might have been borne. But the squeaking and shrieking, the hurrying and scurrying, so that you could neither hear yourself speak nor get a wink of good honest sleep the livelong night! Not to mention that, Mamma must needs sit up, and keep watch and ward over baby's cradle, or there'd have been a big ugly rat running across the poor little fellow's face, and doing who knows what mischief.

Why didn't the good people of the town have cats? Well they did, and there was a fair stand-up fight, but in the end the rats were too many, and the pussies were regularly driven from the field. Poison, I hear you say? Why, they poisoned so many that it fairly bred a plague. Ratcatchers! Why there wasn't a ratcatcher from John o' Groats'

28

House to the Land's End that hadn't
tried his luck. But do what they might,
cats or poison, terrier or traps, there
seemed to be more rats than ever,
and every day a fresh rat was cocking
his tail or pricking his whiskers.

The Mayor and the town council
were at their wits' end. As they were
sitting one day in the town hall racking
their poor brains, and bewailing
their hard fate, who should run in
but the town beadle. "Please your
Honour," says he, "here is a very

queer fellow come to town. I don't rightly
know what to make of him." "Show
him in," said the Mayor, and in he stepped.
A queer fellow, truly. For there wasn't
a colour of the rainbow but you might
find it in some corner of his dress,
and he was tall and thin, and had keen
piercing eyes.

"I'm called the Pied Piper," he began.
"And pray what might you be willing
to pay me, if I rid you of every single
rat in Franchville?"

Well, much as they feared the rats,
they feared parting with their money
more, and fain would they have higgled
and haggled. But the Piper was not a
man to stand nonsense, and the upshot
was that fifty pounds were promised him
(and it meant a lot of money in those
old days) as soon as not a rat was left to
squeak or scurry in Franchville.

Out of the hall stepped the Piper,
and as he stepped he laid his pipe to his
lips and a shrill keen tune sounded
through street and house. And as each
note pierced the air you might have seen
a strange sight. For out of every hole
the rats came tumbling. There were none
too old and none too young, none
too big and none too little to crowd at
the Piper's heels and with eager feet and
upturned noses to patter after him
as he paced the streets. Nor was the Piper
unmindful of the little toddling ones,
for every fifty yards he'd stop and give
an extra flourish on his pipe just to give
them time to keep up with the older
and stronger of the band.

Up Silver Street he went, and
down Gold Street, and at the end of Gold
Street is the harbour and the broad
Solent beyond. And as he paced along,
slowly and gravely, the townsfolk
flocked to door and window, and many
a blessing they called down upon
his head.

As for getting near him there
were too many rats. And now that he
was at the water's edge he stepped into
a boat, and not a rat, as he shoved off
into deep water, piping shrilly all
the while, but followed him, plashing,
paddling, and wagging their tails
with delight. On and on he played and
played until the tide went down,
and each master rat sank deeper and
deeper in the slimy ooze of the harbour,
until every mother's son of them was
dead and smothered.

Do you feel sorry
for the rats?
(Circle your answer.)

YES   NO

Why or why not?

Why have the rats been
able to take over the whole
town?

32

Why do the townspeople
think that the noise the rats
make is worse than the
destruction they cause?

Why are we told that
the rats follow the Piper
"wagging their tails with
delight"?

The tide rose again, and the
Piper stepped on shore, but never a rat
followed. You may fancy the townsfolk
had been throwing up their caps
and hurrahing and stopping up rat-holes
and setting the church bells a-ringing.
But when the Piper stepped ashore
and not so much as a single squeak
was to be heard, the Mayor and the
Council, and the townsfolk generally,
began to hum and to ha and to
shake their heads.

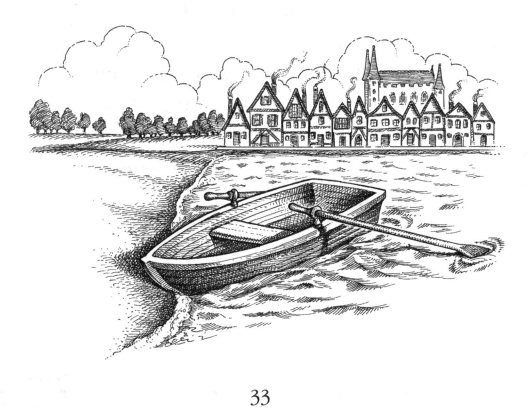

33

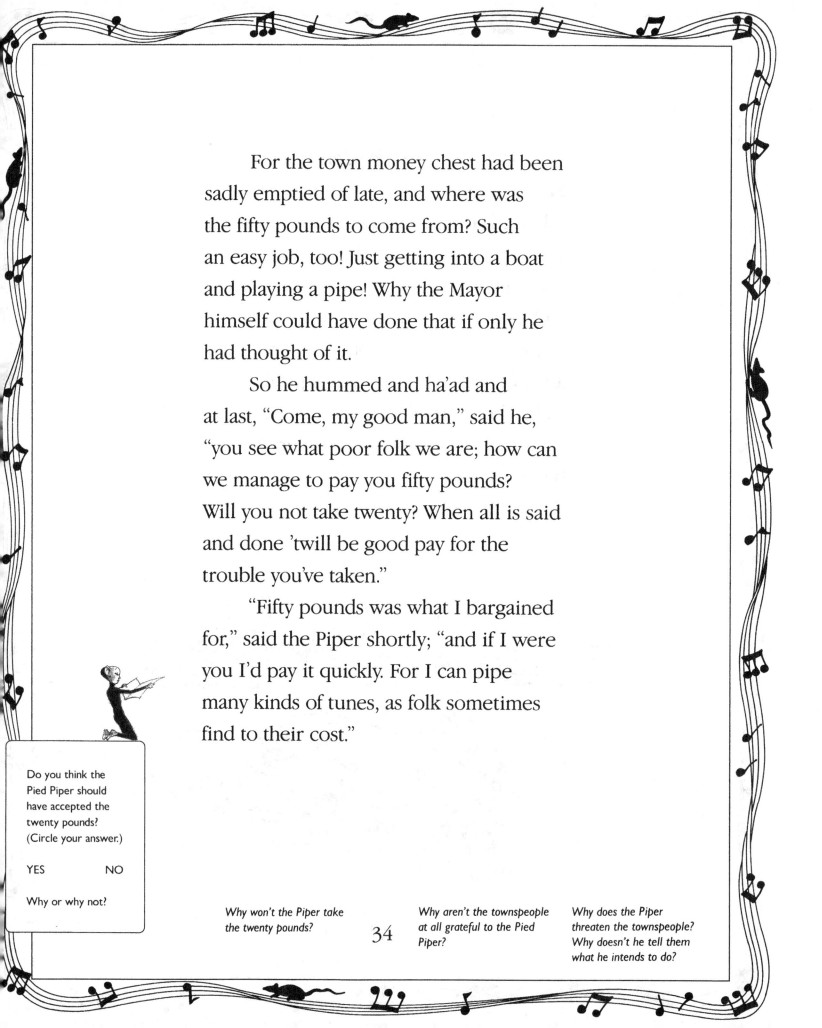

For the town money chest had been
sadly emptied of late, and where was
the fifty pounds to come from? Such
an easy job, too! Just getting into a boat
and playing a pipe! Why the Mayor
himself could have done that if only he
had thought of it.

So he hummed and ha'ad and
at last, "Come, my good man," said he,
"you see what poor folk we are; how can
we manage to pay you fifty pounds?
Will you not take twenty? When all is said
and done 'twill be good pay for the
trouble you've taken."

"Fifty pounds was what I bargained
for," said the Piper shortly; "and if I were
you I'd pay it quickly. For I can pipe
many kinds of tunes, as folk sometimes
find to their cost."

Do you think the
Pied Piper should
have accepted the
twenty pounds?
(Circle your answer.)

YES   NO

Why or why not?

Why won't the Piper take
the twenty pounds?

Why aren't the townspeople
at all grateful to the Pied
Piper?

Why does the Piper
threaten the townspeople?
Why doesn't he tell them
what he intends to do?

"Would you threaten us, you strolling vagabond?" shrieked the Mayor, and at the same time he winked to the Council; "the rats are all dead and drowned," muttered he; and so "You may do your worst, my good man," and with that he turned short upon his heel.

"Very well," said the Piper, and he smiled a quiet smile. With that he laid his pipe to his lips afresh, but now there came forth no shrill notes, as it were, of scraping and gnawing, and squeaking and scurrying, but the tune was joyous and resonant, full of happy laughter and merry play. And as he paced down the streets the elders

mocked, but from schoolroom and
playroom, from nursery and workshop,
not a child but ran out with eager glee
and shout following gaily at the Piper's
call. Dancing, laughing, joining hands
and tripping feet, the bright throng moved
along up Gold Street and down Silver
Street, and beyond Silver Street lay
the cool green forest full of old oaks and
wide-spreading beeches. In and out
among the oak trees you might catch
glimpses of the Piper's many-coloured
coat. You might hear the laughter
of the children break and fade and die

away as deeper and deeper into the lone
green wood the stranger went and
the children followed.

All the while, the elders watched
and waited. They mocked no longer now.
And watch and wait as they might, never
did they set their eyes again upon the
Piper in his parti-coloured coat. Never
were their hearts gladdened by the song
and dance of the children issuing forth
from amongst the ancient oaks of
the forest.

Why don't the townspeople try to stop the children?

Why does the Piper lead the children to a "lone green wood"?

Do you think
the townspeople
deserved to lose
their children?
(Circle your answer.)

YES   NO

Why or why not?

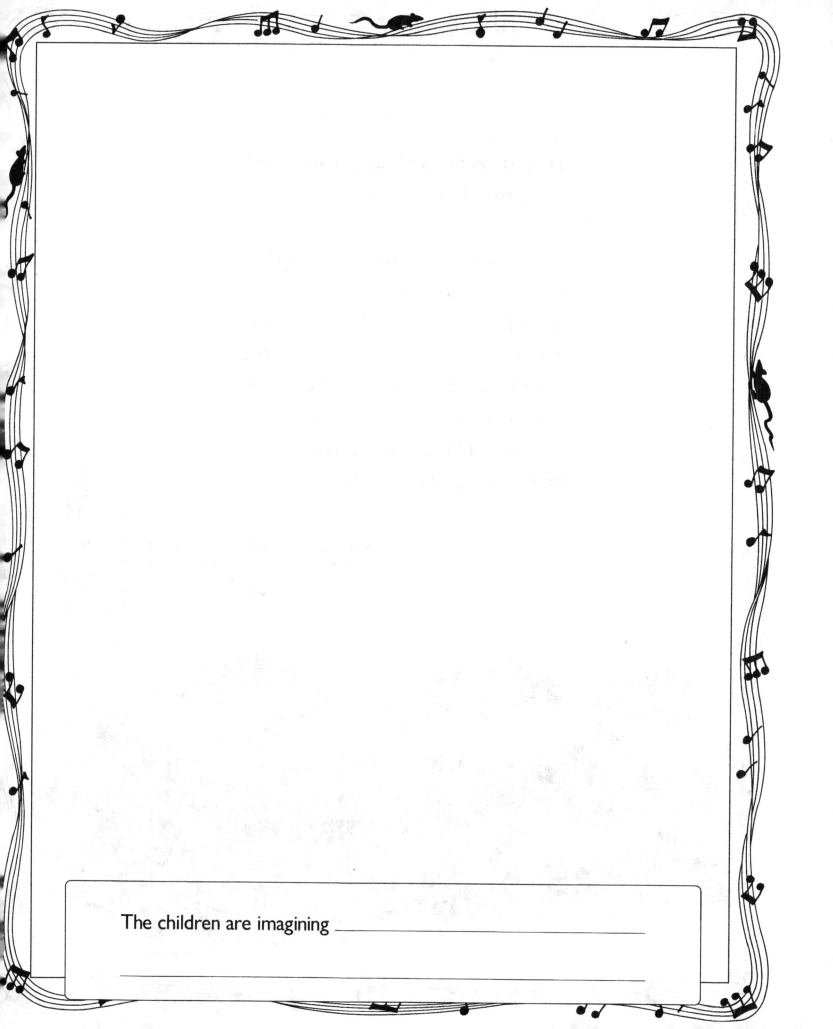

The children are imagining _____

_____

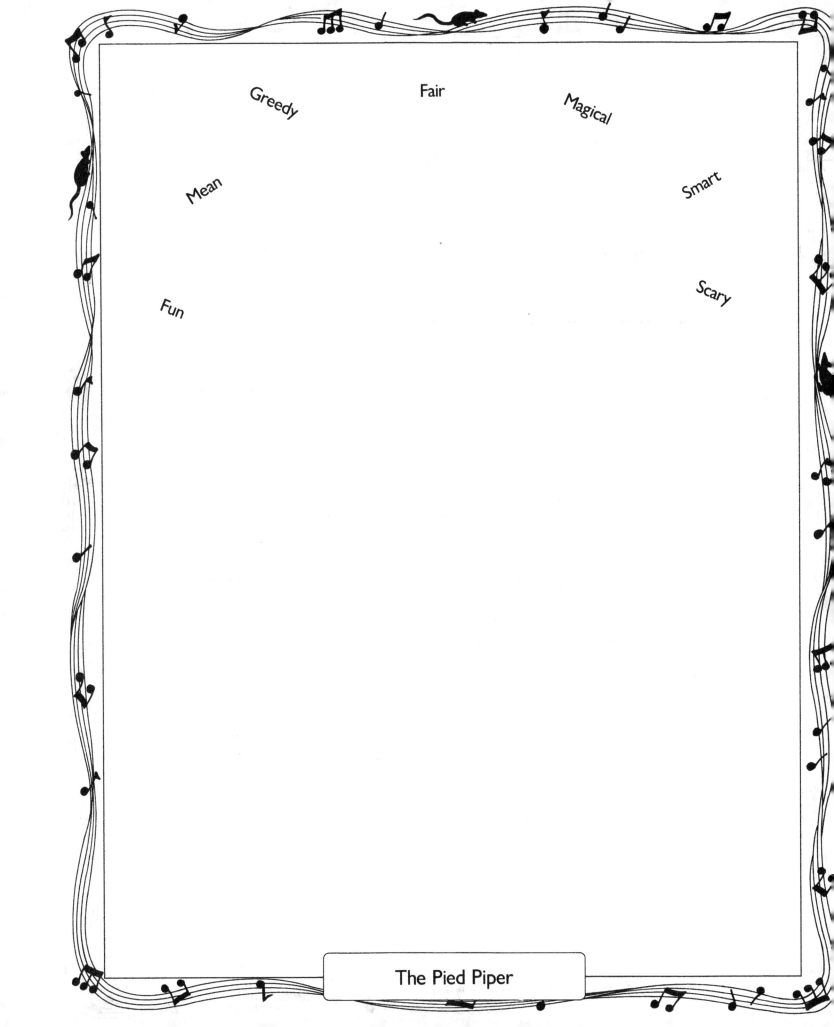

Greedy

Fair

Magical

Mean

Smart

Fun

Scary

The Pied Piper

Song of the Rats

We are the rats!

Listen to the sound of our _____

_____

_____

_____

_____

_____

_____

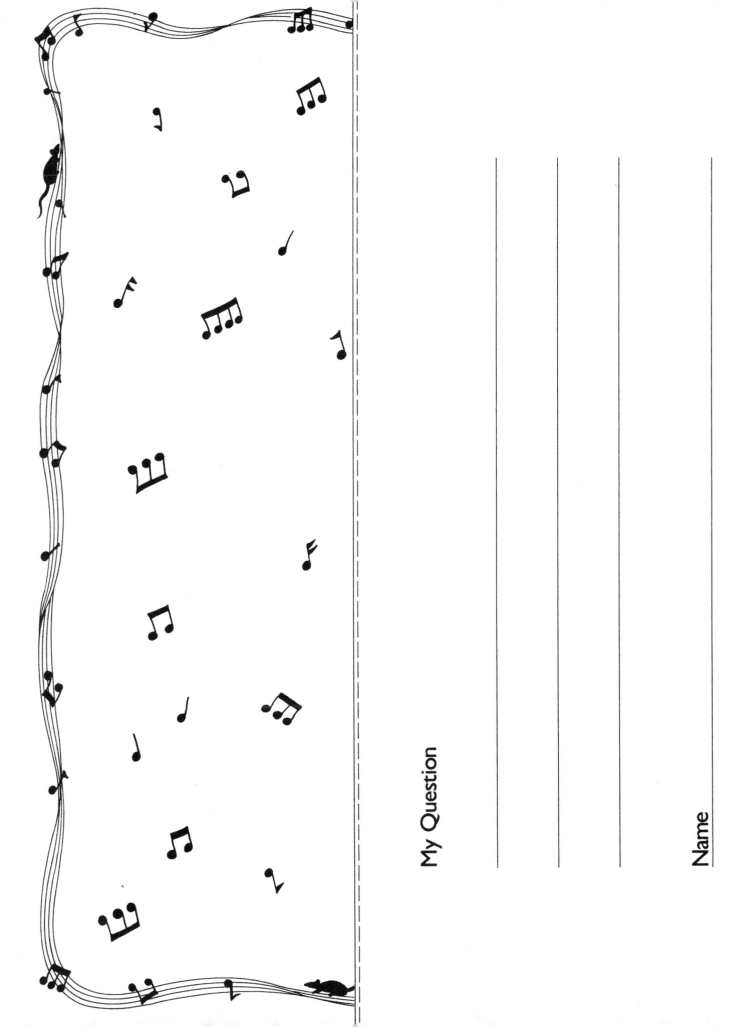

My Question _____

_____

_____

Name _____

FANCIFUL ANIMALS

POETRY BY
EDWARD LEAR
AND
A. A. MILNE

SESSION 1: "The Quangle Wangle's Hat"

This session consists of an introduction and two readings of the poem, a review of the poem's real and imaginary animal names, and an art activity in which children draw their interpretations of the creatures living on the Quangle Wangle's hat.

AT-HOME WORK: "The Quangle Wangle's Hat"

The adult partner reads the poem through once, encouraging the child to join in saying the underlined phrases. The adult then reads the poem a second time, pausing to answer G.B.'s three questions. When called for, children respond to these questions by circling their answer.

After reading, the adult writes the child's own question about "The Quangle Wangle's Hat" into the book.

SESSION 2: "The Quangle Wangle's Hat"

During this reading of the poem, you will collect students' responses to G.B.'s questions and lead a discussion of them. The session concludes with a writing and art activity in which students create names for and draw their own imaginary creatures.

The art activity will be more fun if you have ready a large cutout of the Quangle Wangle's hat (see the illustration for a model) on which to display children's drawings. You might also want to suggest that children bring in materials from home (buttons, bits of ribbon or lace, etc.) to decorate the hat.

SESSION 3: "The Owl and the Pussy-Cat"

This session consists of an introduction and first reading of the poem, a second reading and discussion of the poem, an art activity in which students make masks out of paper plates, and a dramatization and recital of the poem.

For this session you will need to supply paper plates and crayons or markers for the masks. If you wish, you can cut eyeholes in the plates and add pointed ears before distributing the materials.

SESSION 4: "Teddy Bear"

This session consists of an introduction and first reading of the poem, followed by a second reading with textual analysis. This is a long poem, so consider doing the two readings in separate sessions.

SESSION 1 : "The Quangle Wangle's Hat"

INTRODUCTION

Introduce the poem by telling children that "The Quangle Wangle's Hat" includes the names of many different animals, some real and some made up. Explain that the "Crumpetty Tree," where the Quangle Wangle lives, is an imaginary tree, and that the name comes from "crumpet," which is a round, flat cake like a biscuit or an English muffin.

FIRST READING

Have children listen as you read the poem aloud. Before reading the poem a second time, take a few moments to let children ask questions and make comments, and clear up unfamiliar vocabulary, such as "luminous," "fowl," "calf," and "corkscrew."

SECOND READING

Encourage children to follow along in their books as you read the poem aloud a second time. Before you begin, tell children to listen carefully for the names of real and made-up animals. Ask children to join in on the words "Quangle Wangle Quee" at the end of each stanza.

REVIEW OF ANIMAL NAMES

After the second reading, ask children to recall as many real and made-up animal names as they can. Don't be concerned if students miss some real animals or include as real some semi-imaginary ones, such as the Blue Baboon. Write the names on the board and invite suggestions about what children think the made-up animals would look like. Encourage students to consider whether the *sound* of a made-up name, such as "pobble" or "dong," helps them to imagine how the creature might look or move. Make it clear that since these animals are imaginary, everyone's ideas about them will be different.

ART ACTIVITY

After children share a few ideas, have them sketch art notes of a few of their favorite real or imaginary creatures from the poem, using the two spaces below stanzas four and five. As children work, help them find and circle in the text the names of the creatures they are drawing. Allow time for children to share and compare their drawings.

SESSION 2 : "The Quangle Wangle's Hat"

POSTING "MY QUESTIONS"

Have students cut out the questions they wrote at home. Glance through them briefly and note any that you might want to raise during your discussion of G.B.'s questions. Then pin students' questions on the Sharing Questions bulletin board. Let children know that even though there will be no Sharing Questions Discussion this week, they should still look at the bulletin board and talk about their questions with each other.

SESSION 2 : "The Quangle Wangle's Hat" (continued)

READING AND REVIEW OF G.B.'S QUESTIONS

Read the poem aloud, pausing at the end of stanzas two and four to collect responses to G.B.'s first two questions. Ask a few students to act out what the Quangle Wangle said and did when the animals asked if they could live on his hat.

After the reading, discuss G.B.'s last question. Follow up on children's comments with additional questions such as those printed in the margin of your text.

CREATIVE WRITING AND ART ACTIVITY

Tell the class that now they are going to make up their own imaginary creatures. Encourage students to try some of Lear's patterns when thinking of their animals' names—for example, using interesting colors (as in "Golden Grouse" or "Blue Baboon"), similar sounds (as in "Fimble Fowl," "Bisky Bat," or "Quangle Wangle Quee"), or funny characteristics (as in "the Dong with a luminous nose" or "the Pobble who has no toes").

Write the names students offer on the board. Then have students turn to the page captioned "My Made-Up Animal" and write their own made-up animal name (or copy their favorite one from the list on the board) on the line provided. Ask students to draw a picture showing what their animal looks like.

If you wish, students can cut out their completed animals and attach them to a large cutout of the Quangle Wangle's hat. Students may also enjoy decorating the hat, following the description in the first stanza of the poem.

SESSION 3 : "The Owl and the Pussy-Cat"

INTRODUCTION

Introduce the session by telling students that they are going to hear a poem about an owl and a pussy-cat who want to get married. Before the reading, tell students that a "five-pound note" and a "shilling" are British money.

FIRST READING

Have children listen as you read the poem aloud. Before reading the poem a second time, take a few moments to let children ask questions and make comments. Also help children clear up such unfamiliar vocabulary as "mince," "quince," and "runcible spoon," using the definitions given in the margin of your text.

SECOND READING AND DISCUSSION

Read the poem aloud a second time, encouraging children to follow along in their books and to join in saying the last five lines of each stanza.

Afterward, help students think a little more about the poem by asking such questions as *Do you think an owl and a pussy-cat would make a good couple? Why or why not? Why do the Owl and the Pussy-cat sail away to the land where the Bong-tree grows when they decide to get married?*

SESSION 3: "The Owl and the Pussy-Cat" (continued)

ART ACTIVITY

For this activity, you will need to supply each student with drawing materials and a paper plate or piece of heavy paper. Have students make masks by drawing the face of an owl, a pussy-cat, or a piggy-wig on their plates. Remind students that these are pretend animals, who have a pea-green boat, so they may be any color and as fanciful as children like.

DRAMATIZATION AND RECITAL

When the masks are ready, read the poem again, having children wear or hold up their masks and mime the action of the poem. You may want to have children repeat the lines spoken by the character whose mask they are wearing. All can join in on the choruses of stanzas two and three.

SESSION 4: "Teddy Bear"

INTRODUCTION

Introduce the session by telling students that they are going to hear a poem about a teddy bear. Some children will recognize this bear as Winnie-the-Pooh (who sometimes refers to himself as Edward Bear). Explain that in the poem, Teddy is very interested in a picture of King Louis of France, who lived more than two hundred years ago.

FIRST READING

Read the entire poem through once, pausing after stanzas four and eight to ask the questions printed in your text. After the reading, take a few moments to let children ask questions and make comments, and clear up unfamiliar vocabulary. In addition to defining the words printed in the margin of your text, you might want to explain such words and phrases as "clamber," to "grudge" someone something, and "misgiving."

SECOND READING AND TEXTUAL ANALYSIS

Introduce the second reading by telling students to follow along in their books as you read and to join in saying the underlined words and phrases.

During the second reading, pause after stanzas seven and thirteen to conduct a textual analysis, using questions such as those printed in your text. Since the questions after stanza thirteen are interpretive, you may want to extend your discussion of them. Also consider having pairs of students (or the entire class) mime the action of stanzas 8-12 as you read.

FANCIFUL ANIMALS

POETRY

THE
QUANGLE WANGLE'S
HAT

1

On the top of the Crumpetty Tree
    The Quangle Wangle sat,
But his face you could not see,
    On account of his Beaver Hat.
For his Hat was a hundred and two feet wide,
With ribbons and bibbons on every side
And bells, and buttons, and loops, and lace,
So that nobody ever could see the face
    Of the **Quangle Wangle Quee.**

2

The Quangle Wangle said
    To himself on the Crumpetty Tree,
"Jam; and jelly; and bread;
    Are the best food for me!
But the longer I live on this Crumpetty Tree
The plainer than ever it seems to me
That very few people come this way
And that life on the whole is far from gay!"
    Said the **Quangle Wangle Quee.**

3

But there came to the Crumpetty Tree,
    Mr. and Mrs. Canary;
And they said, "Did you ever see
    Any spot so charmingly airy?
May we build a nest on your lovely Hat?
Mr. Quangle Wangle, grant us that!
O please let us come and build a nest
Of whatever material suits you best,
    Mr. **Quangle Wangle Quee!"**

Why doesn't the Quangle Wangle take off his hat? (Circle one.)
1. He's shy
2. Quangle Wangles always wear big hats
3. He's proud of his hat
4. He's afraid
5. The hat is part of his head
6. Other _____
_____
_____

45

4

And besides, to the Crumpetty Tree

    Came the Stork, the Duck, and the Owl;

The Snail, and the Bumble-Bee,

    The Frog, and the Fimble Fowl;

(The Fimble Fowl, with a Corkscrew leg;)

And all of them said, "We humbly beg,

    We may build our homes on your lovely Hat,

Mr. Quangle Wangle, grant us that!

    Mr. **Quangle Wangle Quee!**"

Pretend you are the Quangle Wangle telling the other animals they can live on your hat. What do you think the Quangle Wangle said?

(Have students draw their art notes here.)

5

And the Golden Grouse came there,

    And the Pobble who has no toes,

And the small Olympian bear,

    And the Dong with a luminous nose.

And the Blue Baboon, who played the flute,

And the Orient Calf from the Land of Tute,

And the Attery Squash, and the Bisky Bat,

All came and built on the lovely Hat

    Of the **Quangle Wangle Quee**.

(Have students draw their art notes here.)

6

And the Quangle Wangle said
    To himself on the Crumpetty Tree,
"When all these creatures move
    What a wonderful noise there'll be!"
And at night by the light of the Mulberry moon
They danced to the Flute of the Blue Baboon,
On the broad green leaves of the Crumpetty Tree,
And all were as happy as happy could be,
    With the **Quangle Wangle Quee**.

—Edward Lear

Why does the Quangle Wangle enjoy having a noisy party on his hat?

Why do the creatures want to live on the Quangle Wangle's hat in the first place?

Why does the Quangle Wangle think the noise on his hat is wonderful?

How does the Quangle Wangle feel about not being able to join in the dance?

Why are all the creatures "happy as happy could be" on the Quangle Wangle's hat?

48

My Made-Up Animal

My Question

_____

_____

_____

Name _____

THE OWL
AND THE PUSSY-CAT

1

The Owl and the Pussy-cat went to sea
   In a beautiful pea-green boat,
They took some honey, and plenty of money,
   Wrapped up in a five-pound note.
The Owl looked up to the stars above,
   And sang to a small guitar,
"O lovely Pussy! O Pussy, my love,
   What a beautiful Pussy you are,
      You are,
      You are!
What a beautiful Pussy you are!"

2

Pussy said to the Owl, "You elegant fowl!

    How charmingly sweet you sing!

O let us be married! too long we have tarried:

    But what shall we do for a ring?"

They sailed away, for a year and a day,

    To the land where the Bong-tree grows

And there in a wood a Piggy-wig stood

    With a ring at the end of his nose,

        His nose,

        His nose,

With a ring at the end of his nose.

3

"Dear Pig, are you willing to sell for one shilling
    Your ring?" Said the Piggy, "I will."
So they took it away, and were married next day
    By the Turkey who lives on the hill.
They dined on mince, and slices of quince,
    Which they ate with a runcible spoon;
And hand in hand, on the edge of the sand,
    They danced by the light of the moon,
        The moon,
        The moon,
They danced by the light of the moon.

—Edward Lear

mince: chopped-up food

quince: an exotic fruit

runcible spoon: a word made up by Edward Lear meaning a spoon that has prongs like a fork

TEDDY BEAR

1

A bear, however hard he tries,
Grows tubby without exercise.
Our Teddy Bear is short and fat
Which is not to be wondered at;
He gets what exercise he can
By falling off the ottoman,
But generally seems to lack
The energy to clamber back.

ottoman: a large,
cushioned footstool

2

Now tubbiness is just the thing
Which gets a fellow wondering;
And Teddy worried lots about
The fact that he was rather stout.
He thought: "If only I were thin!
But how does anyone begin?"
He thought: "It really isn't fair
To grudge me exercise and air."

3

For many weeks he pressed in vain
His nose against the window-pane,
And envied those who walked about
Reducing their unwanted stout.
None of the people he could see
"Is quite" (he said) "as fat as me!"
Then, with a still more moving sigh,
"I mean" (he said) "as fat as I!"

4

Now Teddy, as was only right,

Slept in the ottoman at night,

And with him crowded in as well

More animals than I can tell;

Not only these, but books and things,

Such as a kind relation brings—

Old tales of "Once upon a time,"

And history retold in rhyme.

Pause here during your **first** reading and ask:

What is Teddy Bear's problem?

5

One night it happened that he took
A peep at an old picture-book,
Wherein he came across by chance
The picture of a King of France
(A stoutish man) and, down below,
These words: "King Louis So and So,
Nicknamed 'The Handsome!'" There he sat,
*And (think of it!) the man was **fat**!*

6

Our bear rejoiced like anything
To read about this famous King,
Nicknamed "The Handsome." There he sat
And certainly the man was **fat**.
Nicknamed "The Handsome." Not a doubt
The man was definitely **stout**.
Why then, a bear (for all his tub)
Might yet be named "**The Handsome Cub!**"

7

"Might yet be named." Or did he mean
That years ago he "might have been"?
For now he felt a slight misgiving:
"Is Louis So and So still living?
Fashions in beauty have a way
Of altering from day to day.
Is 'Handsome Louis' with us yet?
Unfortunately I forget."

Textual Analysis Questions

Why does Teddy at first think he might yet be named "The Handsome Cub"?

What does Teddy mean when he says, "Fashions in beauty have a way/Of altering from day to day"? Why does Teddy begin to worry that it might no longer be fashionable to be fat?

Why is it important to Teddy to know if King Louis is still around?

8

Next morning (nose to window-pane)
The doubt occurred to him again.
One question hammered in his head:
"Is he alive or is he dead?"
Thus, nose to pane, he pondered; but
The lattice window, loosely shut,
Swung open. With one startled "Oh!"
Our Teddy disappeared below.

Pause here on your **first** reading and ask:

Why is Teddy so interested in King Louis?

9

There happened to be passing by
A plump man with a twinkling eye,
Who, seeing Teddy in the street,
Raised him politely to his feet,
And murmured kindly in his ear
Soft words of comfort and of cheer:
"Well, well!" "Allow me!" "Not at all."
"Tut-tut! A very nasty fall."

10

Our Teddy answered not a word;
It's doubtful if he even heard.
Our bear could only look and look:
The stout man in the picture-book!
That "handsome" King—could this be he,
This man of adiposity?
"Impossible," he thought. "But still,
No harm in asking. Yes I will!"

adiposity: fatness

11

"Are you," he said, "by any chance
His Majesty the King of France?"
The other answered, "I am that,"
Bowed stiffly, and removed his hat;
Then said, "Excuse me," with an air,
"But is it Mr. Edward Bear?"
And Teddy, bending very low,
Replied politely, "Even so!"

12

They stood beneath the window there,
The King and Mr. Edward Bear,
And, handsome, if a trifle fat,
Talked carelessly of this and that…
Then said His Majesty, "Well, well,
I must get on," and rang the bell.
"Your bear, I think," he smiled. "Good-day!"
And turned, and went upon his way.

13

A bear, however hard he tries,

Grows tubby without exercise.

Our Teddy Bear is short and fat,

Which is not to be wondered at.

But do you think it worries him

To know that he is far from slim?

No, just the other way about—

He's *proud* of being short and stout.

—A. A. Milne

Textual Analysis Questions

Why is Teddy Bear proud of being short and stout after he meets the gentleman?

Why does the gentleman tell Teddy that he is the King of France?

Why does Teddy Bear like to be addressed as "Mr. Edward Bear"?

THE MERMAID WHO LOST HER COMB

SCOTTISH FOLKTALE
AS TOLD BY
WINIFRED FINLAY

SESSION 1

INTRODUCTION

Begin the session by telling children that this story takes place in the Outer Hebrides, a group of rocky islands off the coast of Scotland. The boy in the story lives on a *croft*, a small rented farm.

FIRST READING AND SHARING OF RESPONSES

Ask children to listen as you read the story aloud. As you come to the words "peat," "limpet," and "bannock," explain them briefly, using the definitions given in the margin of your text.

After the reading, allow a few moments to clear up unfamiliar vocabulary and to let students ask questions and share their initial reactions to the story. Encourage children to offer their opinions about which parts of the story they especially liked and why.

ART ACTIVITY

Remind children that the boy and the mermaid spend long hours together talking, and that the boy tells her all about his everyday life on the island. Have children turn to the frontispiece and draw a picture showing what they think the mermaid would be most interested in hearing about.

As children draw, circulate among them and help them complete their captions. Allow time for students to share and compare their illustrations.

SESSION 2

POSTING "MY QUESTIONS"

Have students cut out the questions they wrote at home and pin them on the Sharing Questions bulletin board. Children who have not had an at-home reading can dictate their questions to you at this time. Encourage children to look at the Sharing Questions bulletin board during the week, to point out their own questions and to ask about those of their classmates.

READING AND REVIEW OF G.B.'S QUESTIONS

Read the story aloud, encouraging children to follow along in their books. Pause to collect students' responses to G.B.'s questions (pages 10, 18, and 26). Help students think further about the friendship between the boy and the mermaid and about why Haskeir is the best place for them to live together by asking additional questions such as those given in the margin of your text.

SESSION 2 (continued)

ART ACTIVITY

Ask children to turn to the page captioned "The boy loves the mermaid because…" and have them draw a picture of the mermaid showing what the boy likes best about her. As children draw, circulate among them and help them complete their captions. Allow time for students to share and compare their drawings.

SESSION 3

SHARING QUESTIONS DISCUSSION

Prepare for discussion as usual, deciding on the five or six interpretive questions you intend to ask the class. Note which of the children's questions are similar to those you plan to lead and try to include three or four of their questions in your final list. When you write your questions on the board, include children's names as appropriate.

Suggested Interpretive Questions

Why does the love in the boy's heart make the comb magic?

Why does the boy need the Wise Woman to tell him that the comb is magic?

Why does the mermaid stop being "careless" when she gets the new comb?

Why does the Sea-king, unlike the boy's mother, approve of the marriage?

ART ACTIVITY

Introduce the activity by reminding students that the young man and the mermaid cannot live together in his mother's house, so the Sea-king gives them an island of their own to live on. Ask students to recall their answers to G.B.'s third question ("Why is Haskeir the perfect home for the young man and the mermaid?"). Briefly discuss what life is like on the island and why they think the couple is happy there. Then ask students to draw a picture of life on the island. Allow time for them to share and compare their illustrations.

SESSION 4

GROUP CREATIVE WRITING

Write on the board the title "Comb Poem" and copy the outline given in the student book. Remind students that the love in the boy's heart is what makes the comb magic. Ask them to imagine what the boy might be thinking about as he works on the comb. For example, he might think about what he likes best about the mermaid, how he feels about making the comb for her, or how he hopes she will respond when he gives her the comb.

Explain to students that, to give their poem the shape of a comb, they are going to alternate long lines and short lines. You might suggest some patterns they could adopt. For example, the long lines might be complete thoughts, and the short lines might add brief descriptive details or repeat key words from the preceding line.

Write students' suggestions on the board to fill out the comb outline. When the poem is finished, read it back to the class. Make copies for students to paste in their books on the page provided, or have them copy the poem themselves.

Here is an example of a poem that a class might compose:

Comb Poem

The mermaid's lovely hair flows
like waves.
I long to be her friend,
her friend.
I hope she will be happy with
this comb,
and let me be her friend forever.

THE MERMAID WHO LOST HER COMB

SCOTTISH FOLKTALE

The mermaid is interested in _____

_____

Many, many years ago, on the island of North Uist, in the Outer Hebrides, there lived a poor widow with seven children. The work of the croft fell chiefly on the eldest boy who spent long hours cultivating their little plot of ground, cutting and stacking peat for the fire and, whenever the weather allowed, putting out to sea to catch fish to feed all the hungry mouths.

Uist: pronounced "you-ist"

croft: a small rented farm

peat: chunks of dried moss and plants that are burned for fuel

There was no time for him to play
with boys of his own age, even
with his little brothers and sisters,
but because he loved his mother dearly,
he was pleased to help her in any way
that he could.

Now one afternoon, when the
work of the croft was done, the boy
hurried down to the little sandy bay
where his boat was beached, put
aboard his nets, and rowed out to sea,
thinking how splendid it would be if he
could catch a fine salmon, or perhaps
a young trout, or even some delicious
herring.

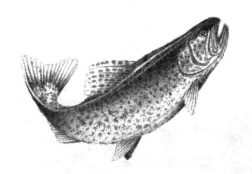

When he had shot his nets,
he rowed back to the island and began
to search the rocky foreshore for
oysters and scallops, crabs and whelks.
Presently, above the thud and swish
of the breaking waves, he heard a new
sound, as though someone were crying.
Rounding a rocky headland, he came
upon a little mermaid sitting on a rock,
the tears falling from her sea-green eyes,
trickling down her cheeks to
splash like rain in the pool beside her,
while a wise old limpet made soothing
noises, but brought his shell down sharply
as soon as he saw the boy.

limpet: a small shellfish that clings to rocks

9

Why is the boy the kind of person you would want as a friend? (Underline some things on these two pages that help you answer this question.)

Why does the boy stop searching for food to look for the mermaid's comb?

Why does the boy offer to make the mermaid a new comb?

Why is the boy so sure he will be able to make a mermaid's comb?

"Why," exclaimed the boy, "whatever is the matter? Is there not enough salt in the sea, without your adding to it with your tears?"

The little mermaid looked through her tangled yellow hair and twitched her shining tail. "How can I help but weep?" she asked. "I have lost my comb and I can not tidy my hair."

She began to cry again, so that the tears splashed like rain into the pool beside her, and the limpet made muffled, reassuring noises from inside his tightly closed shell.

"Lost your comb?" the boy repeated. "Is that such a serious matter that you have to cry so bitterly?"

"Of course it is serious," the little mermaid answered. "You see, it was a magic comb, made by a mortal between sunset and dawn. My father will be very angry when he knows I have lost it. I am always losing things," she added sadly.

10

"I am afraid I am a very careless
little mermaid."

"Have you any idea where you
lost it?" the boy asked, knowing that he
ought to be hunting for food for
his mother and brothers and sisters
instead of helping a careless mermaid
to find her comb.

"Somewhere on these rocks," the
mermaid answered, cheering up as the boy
started to search in all the crevices and
cracks, lifting up stones and replacing them,
so that the sea creatures which sheltered
underneath should not be disturbed.

But there was no comb to be
found anywhere.

"I'll tell you what I'll do," the
boy said, as the mermaid began to look
as though at any moment she would
start crying again. "Tonight I shall make
you a new comb, and if you will meet me
here at the same time tomorrow afternoon,
I shall be waiting with it for you."

"Oh, thank you," the little mermaid cried, clapping her hands joyfully. "I shall be here. I promise."

She slipped off her rock into the sea, her tangled yellow hair floating around her and her shining green-gold tail flashing in the water, and the next moment she was gone.

"It should not be too difficult to make a comb," the boy thought, "but for it to be magic, I must consult the Wise Woman of North Uist. There is no time to lose, as the sun will soon be setting."

Slowly he walked back along
the beach, searching until he found three
razor shells which he put in his pocket,
and then he found a splendid, fat lobster
which he bore home in triumph for his
mother to cook for their supper.

When everyone was asleep that
night, he got up and tip-toed out
of the cottage and into the moonlight,
and sitting down with his back against the
little haystack which was to feed their
donkey, he took out his knife and the
first of the razor shells, and began to
fashion a comb. When it was half-done,
and he was beginning to congratulate
himself on his skill, the shell broke
in two and he had to throw it away.

He started to work on the second
shell, and when it was two-thirds done,
and he was beginning to congratulate
himself on his skill, the shell broke
in two and he had to throw it away.

Realizing now how difficult it was
to make a comb for a mermaid, he took
the third shell from his pocket,
and concentrating on the work so that
he had no time to congratulate himself
at all, he fashioned a comb which
was perfect.

"Now I must ask the Wise Woman
how to make it a magic comb," he
thought, and he ran through the
moonlight to the furthermost cottage
where the Wise Woman lived, and
he knocked on her door.

"Who is it that knocks so late on my cottage door?" the Wise Woman asked.

"I am my mother's eldest son," the boy answered. "I have fashioned a comb for a mermaid and now I wish to buy some magic for it."

Opening the door, the Wise Woman looked first at the boy, and then at the comb, and finally she smiled.

"You do not need my help, eldest son. The love in your heart put magic in your fingers so that the comb became magic the moment you finished it."

Thanking her, the boy ran home, tumbled into bed and slept for half-an-hour before the cock crowed to announce the new day. Hastily he got up and ran down to the strand, yawning because he was so tired. Putting out his boat, he jumped in and rowed to where he had shot his nets, but when he pulled them aboard, there was only one dogfish, and he knew that he would have to go hungry as well as sleepless that day.

In the afternoon, when he had
finished working on the croft,
he returned to the rocky headland,
and was delighted to find the little
mermaid was already sitting on her
rock, the breeze playing with her
tangled yellow hair.

So pleased was she with the comb
he had carved for her that he forgot he
had had but little sleep and that his
brothers and sisters had eaten all of the
dogfish—and asked for more.

Why is the mermaid the kind of person you would want as a friend? (Underline some things on these two pages that help you answer this question.)

Why does the mermaid tell the boy that she is the Sea-king's daughter? Why didn't she tell him before?

Why doesn't the boy believe what the mermaid tells him about catching the fish?

Why is the mermaid all the more pleased to see the boy after he has missed a day? Why isn't she annoyed or hurt?

"I am the Sea-king's daughter," the mermaid said, combing her yellow hair with her new comb, "and my comb, which was once a razor shell, tells me that you had but little sleep last night and nothing to eat today."

"I shall have bannocks tonight," the boy answered, "and I shall sleep soundly, and tomorrow I may be lucky and find more fish in my nets."

bannocks: oatmeal biscuits

"Follow me, and shoot your nets when I tell you," the mermaid said, diving into the sea. At once the boy launched his boat and rowed after her, and when she signalled, he shot his nets.

"Now lift them," the mermaid ordered.

"But they have to be left overnight," the boy protested.

"Do as I say," the mermaid commanded.

"It won't be any use," the boy argued, but when he bent to pull his nets,

18

they were so heavy with fish that he could scarcely haul them on board.

From that time on, he always found his nets full of fish, so that there were second helpings—yes—and third helpings too, of fine trout and salmon for the whole family.

Because the mermaid filled his nets for him, he had more time to spare than before, and so each day he would hurry to the headland where the mermaid would be waiting for him, and they would sit and talk about everything on earth—and in the sea too.

So the days became weeks, the weeks months, and the months years, and though there were times when the boy was too busy on the croft, cutting peat for the fire, making hay, harvesting the oats, or planting seeds, the mermaid always understood and was all the more pleased to see him the next day.

At last the time came when the boy was no longer a boy, but a strong and handsome young man, who spoke but little and sighed a great deal.

"Why," exclaimed the mermaid one day, "whatever is the matter? Is there not enough wind on North Uist without your adding to it with your sighs?"

"I sigh because all these long years I have loved you. I want to make you my wife, but it will be a long time before I can ask you, because I must wait until my brother is old enough to do my work on the croft, and care for my mother, as I have done."

"I can wait," the mermaid said, for she knew that the only person she wanted to marry was the boy who had made her the comb when she was a little mermaiden.

At long last the time came when
the brother was old enough to take over
the croft and care for his mother
and brothers and sisters, and the boy,
who was now a young man, told
his mother that the time had come for
him to marry and to bring home
his bride. When his mother heard that
it was a mermaid that her son wished to
marry, she was very angry.

"No good will come of such
a marriage," she cried. "Is there no girl
on the island to make you a good wife?"
Though he argued and reasoned with
her all day and all night, she refused to
welcome the mermaid into her home.

Sadly the young man went down to
the shore where the mermaid awaited
him. Sadly he told her that there was no
welcome for her in his mother's house.

"We must ask the help of my father,
the Sea-king," the mermaid decided,
and she sent a message by a flounder
who happened to be passing. Almost
immediately a foam-crested wave
appeared on the horizon and rolled in
towards the island, and now the young

man could see the Sea-king in his chariot which was drawn by eight white horses with tossing white manes.

"Father," said the mermaid, "this is the crofter of North Uist who carved me a comb when he was a boy and when I was a little mermaiden. All these years we have loved each other, but now that it is possible for us to marry, there is no welcome for me in his mother's home."

"Your mother is wiser than you realize," the Sea-king said to the young man. "There would be no peace where one roof sheltered a woman of the island and a woman of the sea. You must have a cottage and a croft of your own."

"I have no money to buy a croft, and I could not rent one, because the Steward of the island is a friend of my mother's, and she will see that he does not let me have any land."

"North Uist is not the only place in the world," the Sea-king pointed out.

Slowly turning round to face the sea, he started to sing in a strange tongue. Immediately the waters began to churn and boil, throwing up huge veils of spray: the sky darkened as though it were night and a great flash of lightning accompanied by a crack of thunder made the young man shiver.

The next moment it was daylight
again and the sun was shining, but where
there had been only blue-grey sea with
its white-capped waves now there
was a rocky island, and on its shores
a host of grey seals basked and played
and slumbered.

"Here is your own island," the
Sea-king said. "It is called Haskeir.
The seals will guard both it and you.
They will permit those who are your
friends to land on it, but they will
not allow anyone to set foot on it
without your consent."

So the young man and the mermaid
were married and lived happily ever after
on the island of Haskeir, and they had
many children who were as good and
kind as their parents.

When the widow saw what a splendid
wife and mother the mermaid was,
she admitted she had made a mistake.

"Nothing but good has come
of this marriage," she said, and her
greatest happiness was when the
grey seals pulled her boat over the sea
to Haskeir, and she sat with her son
and his wife, rocking the cradle in which
the youngest child slept, and watching
the others laughing and playing in the
sun-warmed pools and crevices
of the rocks.

Why is Haskeir the
perfect home for
the young man and
the mermaid?

*What would the
mermaid like best
about Haskeir?*

*What would the
young man like best
about Haskeir?*

26

The young man and the mermaid are happy on Haskeir because

_____

The boy loves the mermaid because _____

_____

Comb Poem

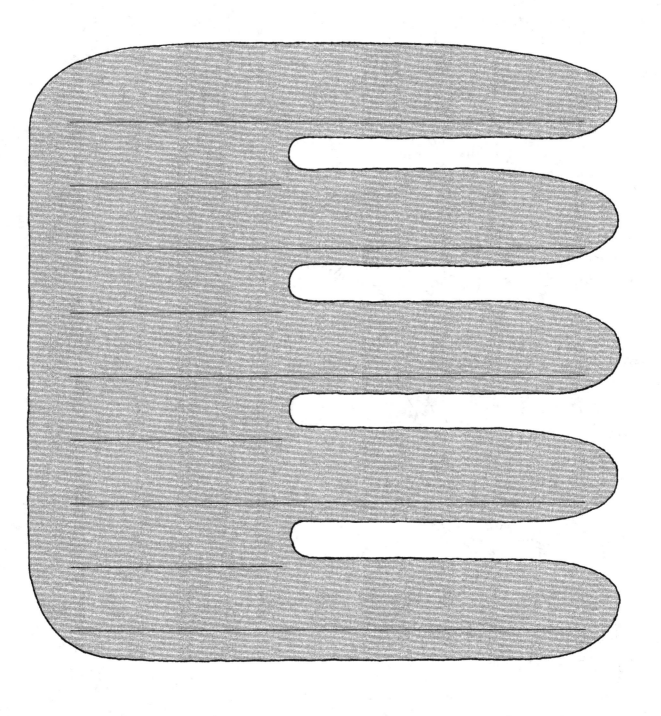

My Question

Name

HANSEL AND GRETEL

BROTHERS GRIMM,
TRANSLATED BY
RANDALL JARRELL

SESSION 1

This session consists of an introduction and first reading of the story, followed by a brief sharing of questions and comments, and an art activity in which children draw their interpretation of the witch's house.

AT-HOME WORK

During this second reading of the story, the adult partner encourages the child to join in saying the underlined phrases, and pauses to discuss G.B.'s three questions. When called for, children respond to these questions by underlining parts of the story or by circling either "yes" or "no."

After reading, the adult writes the child's own question about the story into the book in preparation for the Sharing Questions Discussion (Session 4).

SESSION 2

During this reading of the story, you will collect students' responses to G.B.'s questions and lead a discussion of them. The session concludes with an art activity in which children draw the bravest thing they think Hansel does.

SESSION 3

In this session, children act out the story and discuss their interpretations of the characters.

SESSION 4

This session consists of a Sharing Questions Discussion and an art activity in which children draw the bravest thing they think Gretel does.

SESSION 1

INTRODUCTION

Begin the session by telling students that they are going to hear a story about a boy named Hansel and his sister, Gretel. Explain that at the beginning of the story there is a great *famine* in the land—a time when there is very little food available for people to eat.

FIRST READING AND SHARING OF RESPONSES

Ask children to listen as you read the story aloud. After the reading, allow a few moments to clear up unfamiliar vocabulary and to let students ask questions and share their initial reactions to the story. Encourage children to offer their opinions about which parts of the story they liked the most or found the scariest, and why.

ART ACTIVITY

Have children create the story's frontispiece by asking them to draw the witch's bread house with its roof of cake and windows of transparent sugar-candy. Allow time for students to share and compare their illustrations.

SESSION 2

POSTING "MY QUESTIONS"

Have students cut out the questions they wrote at home and pin them on the Sharing Questions bulletin board. Children who have not had an at-home reading can dictate their questions to you at this time. Encourage children to look at the Sharing Questions bulletin board during the week, to point out their own questions and to ask about those of their classmates.

READING AND REVIEW OF G.B.'S QUESTIONS

Read the story aloud, encouraging children to follow along in their books. Pause to collect students' responses to G.B.'s questions (pages 44, 48, and 55). Encourage children to elaborate on their answers by asking additional questions such as those given in the margin of your text.

ART ACTIVITY

Have children turn to the page at the end of the story captioned "The bravest thing Hansel did was...." Ask a few students for their opinions before children begin their drawings. As students work, circulate among them and help them complete their captions. Allow time for students to share and compare their pictures.

SESSION 3

DRAMATIZATION

Tell the class that they are going to act out part of the story. If your class is experienced in performing dramatizations, consider acting out the story twice, using two different groups of actors, so that students can compare different ways of playing the characters.

Assign the parts: Hansel, Gretel, the father, the stepmother, the snow-white bird, and the witch. Also assign children to be trees, beasts and birds of the forest, and the witch's house; ask them to set the moods for their scenes.

After assigning parts, briefly review the incidents of the story, beginning with the first time Hansel and Gretel's parents take them out to the forest, and ending with the death of the witch. Then ask students to act out Hansel and Gretel's adventures.

After the dramatization, conduct a brief discussion on the character interpretations. If you have had two performances, discuss any differences students may have noted. Ask such questions as *Why does the father agree to leave Hansel and Gretel in the forest if he feels sorry for them? Why do Hansel and Gretel follow the snow-white bird? Why does the witch at first pretend to be friendly? How does Gretel feel when she finds out that the witch is planning to eat her, too?*

SESSION 4

SHARING QUESTIONS DISCUSSION

Prepare for discussion as usual, deciding on the five or six interpretive questions you intend to ask the class. Note which of the children's questions are similar to those you plan to lead and try to include three or four of their questions in your final list. When you write your questions on the board, include children's names as appropriate.

Suggested Interpretive Questions

Why is Hansel able to comfort Gretel?

Why is Gretel finally able to kill the witch?

Why is Gretel the one who figures out the way to get across the pond? Why does she know that the duck can only carry them across one at a time?

SESSION 4 (continued)

ART ACTIVITY

Have children turn to the page captioned "The bravest thing Gretel did was...."
Ask a few students for their opinions before children begin their drawings.
As students work, circulate among them and help them complete their
captions. Allow time for students to share and compare their pictures.

HANSEL AND GRETEL

BROTHERS GRIMM

The Witch's House

Once upon a time, on the edge of a
great forest, there lived a poor woodcutter
with his wife and his two children.
The boy was named Hansel and the girl
was named Gretel. The family had
little enough to eat, and once when there
was a great famine in the land the man
could no longer even get them their daily
bread. One night, lying in bed thinking,
in his worry he kept tossing and turning,
and sighed, and said to his wife: "What is
going to become of us? How can we feed
our poor children when we don't even
have anything for ourselves?"

"You know what, husband?"
answered the wife. "The first thing in the
morning we'll take the children out
into the forest, to the thickest part of all.

There we'll make them a fire and give
each of them a little piece of bread; then
we'll go off to our work and leave
them there alone. They won't be able
to find their way back home, and we'll
have got rid of them for good."

"No, wife," said the man, "I won't do
it. How could I have the heart to leave
my children alone in the forest—in no
time the wild beasts would come and tear
them to pieces."

"Oh, you fool!" said she. "Then all four of us will starve to death—you may as well start planing the planks for our coffins," and she gave him no peace until he agreed. "I do feel sorry for the poor children, though," said the man.

The two children hadn't been able to go to sleep either, they were so hungry, and they heard what their stepmother said to their father. Gretel cried as if her heart would break, and said to Hansel: "We're as good as dead." "Ssh! Gretel," said Hansel, "don't you worry, I'll find some way to help us." And as soon as the old folks had gone to sleep, he got up, put on his little coat, opened the bottom half of the door, and slipped out. The moon was shining bright as day, and the white pebbles that lay there in front of the house glittered like new silver coins. Hansel stooped over and put as many as he could into his coat pocket. Then he went back in again, and said to Gretel: "Don't you feel bad, dear little sister! You just go to sleep. God will take care of us." Then he lay down in his bed again.

The next morning, before the sun had risen, the woman came and woke the two children: "Get up, you lazy creatures, we're going to the forest and get wood." Then she gave each of them a little piece of bread and said: "There is something for your dinner, but don't you eat it before, because it's all you're going to get." Gretel put the bread in her apron, since Hansel had the pebbles in his pocket. Then they all started out together on the way to the forest. After they had been walking a little while Hansel stopped and looked back at the house, and did it again and again. His father said: "Hansel, what

are you looking at? What are you hanging
back there for? Watch out or you'll
forget your legs."

"Oh, Father," said Hansel, "I'm
looking at my little white pussycat that's
sitting on the roof and wants to say
goodbye to me."

The wife said: "Fool, that's not your
pussycat, that's the morning sun shining
on the chimney." But Hansel hadn't
been looking back at the cat—every
time he'd stopped he'd dropped onto
the path one of the white pebbles from
his pocket.

When they came to the middle of
the forest the father said: "Now get
together some wood, children! I'll light
you a fire, so you won't be cold."
Hansel and Gretel pulled together
brushwood till it was as high as a little
mountain. The wood was lighted,
and when the flames were leaping high,
the woman said: "Now lie down by
the fire, children, and take a rest, we're
going into the forest to cut wood.
When we're finished we'll come back
and get you."

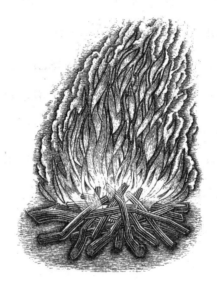

Hansel and Gretel sat by the fire,
and when noon came they each ate
their little piece of bread. And since
they heard the blows of the ax, they
thought their father was near. But it
wasn't the ax, it was a branch that
he'd fastened to a dead tree so that the
wind would blow it back and forth.
And when they'd been sitting there a long
time, they got so tired that their eyes
closed, and they fell fast asleep. When at
last they woke up, it was pitch black.
Gretel began to cry, and said: "Now how
will we ever get out of the forest?"
But Hansel comforted her: "Just wait
awhile till the moon comes up, then we'll
be able to find our way." And when
the full moon had risen, Hansel took his

little sister by the hand and followed
the pebbles, that glittered like new silver
coins and showed them the way.

They walked the whole night
through, and just as the day was breaking
they came back to their father's house.
They knocked on the door, and when
the woman opened it and saw that
it was Hansel and Gretel, she said:
"You bad children, why did you sleep
so long in the forest? We thought
you weren't coming back at all."

But the father was very glad, for it had almost broken his heart to leave them behind alone.

Not long afterwards there was again a famine throughout the land, and the children heard their mother saying to their father in bed one night: "Everything's eaten again. We've only a half a loaf left, and that will be the end of us. The children must go. We'll take them deeper into the forest, so that this time they won't find their way back; it's our only chance." The man's heart was heavy, and he thought: "It would be better for you to share the last bite of food with your children." But the woman wouldn't listen to what he had to say, but scolded him and reproached him. If you say "A" then you have to say "B" too, and since he had given in the first time, he had to give in the second time too.

On these two pages, underline some things that happen to Hansel and Gretel that you think are scary.

How do you think Hansel feels when he finds out that the stepmother has locked the door?

Why does Hansel tell his father that he is looking back at his pigeon who wants to say goodbye to him?

Why do Hansel and Gretel stay by the fire when they know their parents aren't coming back for them?

But the children were still awake, and had heard what was said. As soon as the old folks were asleep, Hansel got up again to go out and pick up pebbles as he'd done the time before, but the woman had locked the door, and Hansel couldn't get out. He comforted his little sister, though, and said: "Don't cry, Gretel, but just go to sleep. The good Lord will surely take care of us."

Early in the morning the woman came and got the children out of their beds. She gave them their little piece of bread, but this time it was even smaller than the time before. On the way to the forest Hansel broke up the bread in his pocket, and often would stop and scatter the crumbs on the ground. "Hansel, what are you stopping and looking back for?" said the father. "Come on!"

44

"I'm looking at my little pigeon that's sitting on the roof and wants to say goodbye to me," answered Hansel.

"Fool," said the woman, "that isn't your pigeon, that's the morning sun shining on the chimney." But Hansel, little by little, scattered all the crumbs on the path.

The woman led the children still deeper into the forest, where they'd never been before in all their lives. Then there was again a great fire made, and the mother said: "Just sit there, children, and if you get tired you can take a nap. We're going into the forest to cut wood, and this evening when we're finished we'll come and get you."

When it was noon, Gretel shared her bread with Hansel, who'd scattered his along the way. Then they fell asleep, and the afternoon went by, but no one came to the poor children.

They didn't wake until it was pitch black, and Hansel comforted his little sister, and said: "Just wait till the moon comes up, Gretel, then we'll see the bread crumbs I scattered. They'll show us the way home." When the moon rose they started out, but they didn't find any crumbs, for the many thousands of birds that fly about in the fields and in the forest had picked them all up. Hansel said to Gretel: "Surely we'll find the way." But they didn't find it. They walked all that night and all the next day, from morning to evening, but they never did get out of the forest. And they were so hungry, for they'd had nothing to eat but a few berries they found on the ground. And when they got so tired that their legs wouldn't hold them up any longer, they lay down under a tree and fell asleep.

By now it was already the third morning since they'd left their father's house. They started to go on again, but they kept getting deeper and deeper into the forest, and unless help came soon they must die of hunger. When it was noon, they saw a beautiful snow-white bird, sitting on a bough, who sang so beautifully that they stood still and listened to him. As soon as he had finished he spread his wings and flew off ahead of them, and they followed him till they came to a little house. The bird perched on the roof of it, and when they got up close to it they saw that the little house was made of bread and the roof was made of cake; the windows, though, were made out of transparent sugar-candy.

"We'll get to work on that," said Hansel, "and have a real feast. I'll eat a piece of the roof. Gretel, you can eat some of the window—that will taste sweet!" Hansel reached up and broke off a little of the roof, to see how it tasted, and Gretel went up to the windowpane and nibbled at it. Then a shrill voice called out from inside the house:

> "Nibble, nibble, little mouse,
> Who is gnawing at my house?"

The children answered:

> "It is not I, it is not I—
> It is the wind, the child of the sky,"

and they went on eating without stopping. The roof tasted awfully good to Hansel, so he tore off a great big piece of it, and Gretel pushed out a whole round windowpane, and sat down and really enjoyed it.

If you were Hansel or Gretel, would *you* keep on eating the house after hearing the voice inside? (Circle your answer.)

YES   NO

Why or why not?

Why do Hansel and Gretel keep on eating the house after hearing the voice inside?

48

Why do Hansel and Gretel answer the witch by saying, "It is not I,...it is the wind, the child of the sky"?

All at once the door opened,
and a woman as old as the hills, leaning
on crutches, came creeping out.
Hansel and Gretel were so frightened
that they dropped what they had
in their hands. But the old woman just
nodded her head and said: "My, my, you
dear children, who has brought you
here? Come right in and stay with me.
No harm will befall you." She took both
of them by the hand and led them into her
little house. Then she set nice food
before them—milk and pancakes with
sugar, apples and nuts. After that

she made up two beautiful white beds
for them, and Hansel and Gretel
lay down in them and thought they
were in heaven.

But the old woman had only
pretended to be so friendly; really she
was a wicked witch who lay in wait
for children, and had built the house of
bread just to lure them inside. When
one came into her power she would kill
it, cook it, and eat it, and that would
be a real feast for her. Witches have red
eyes and can't see far, but they have a
keen sense of smell, like animals,
so that they can tell whenever human
beings get near. As Hansel and Gretel
had got close the witch had given
a wicked laugh, and had said mockingly:
"Now I've got them. This time they
won't get away."

Early in the morning, before
the children were awake, she was already
up, and when she saw both of them
fast asleep and looking so darling, with
their rosy fat cheeks, she muttered to
herself: "That will be a nice bite!" Then she
seized Hansel with her shriveled hands
and shut him up in a little cage with
a grating in the lid, and locked it;
and scream as he would, it didn't help
him any. Then she went to Gretel,
shook her till she woke up, and cried:
"Get up, you lazy creature, fetch
some water and cook your brother
something good. He has to stay in the
cage and get fat. As soon as he's fat
I'll eat him." Gretel began to cry as if
her heart would break, but it was all
no use. She had to do what the wicked
witch told her to do.

Now the finest food was cooked
for poor Hansel, but Gretel got nothing
but crab shells. Every morning the
old woman would creep out to the cage
and cry: "Hansel, put your finger out so
I can feel whether you are getting fat."
But Hansel would put out a bone,
and the old woman's eyes were so bad
that she couldn't tell that, but thought it
was Hansel's finger, and she just couldn't
understand why he didn't get fat.

When four weeks had gone by
and Hansel still was as thin as ever,
she completely lost patience, and was
willing to wait no longer. "Come on,
Gretel, hurry up and get some water!
Whether he's fat or whether he's thin,
tomorrow I'll kill Hansel and cook him."

Oh, how the poor little sister
did grieve as she had to get the water,
and how the tears ran down her cheeks!
"Dear Lord, help us now!" she cried out.

"If only the wild beasts in the forest had eaten us, then at least we'd have died together."

"Stop making all that noise," said the old woman. "It won't help you one bit."

Early the next morning Gretel had to go out and fill the kettle with water and light the fire. "First we'll bake," said the old woman. "I've already heated the oven and kneaded the dough." She pushed poor Gretel up to the oven, out of which the flames were already shooting up fiercely. "Crawl in," said the witch, "and see whether it's got hot enough for us to put the bread in." And when Gretel was in, she'd close the oven and Gretel would be baked, and then she'd eat her too. But Gretel saw what she was up to, and said: "I don't know how to. How do I get inside?"

"Goose, goose!" cried the witch,
"the oven is big enough—why, look, I can
even get in myself," and she scrambled
up and stuck her head in the oven.
Then Gretel gave her a push, so that
she fell right in, and Gretel shut the
door and fastened the bolt. Oh, then she
began to howl in the most dreadful way
imaginable, but Gretel ran away, and the
wicked witch burned to death miserably.

But Gretel ran to Hansel as fast
as she could, opened the cage,
and cried: "Hansel, we are saved!
The old witch is dead!" Hansel sprang
out like a bird from its cage when the
door was opened. How they did rejoice,
and throw their arms around each
other's necks, and dance around and kiss
each other! And since there wasn't
anything to fear, now, they went into the
witch's house, and in every corner
of it stood chests of pearls and precious
stones. "These are even better than
pebbles," said Hansel, and stuck into his
pocket as many as he could; and
Gretel said, "I'll take some home too,"
and filled her apron full.

Why do Hansel and
Gretel want to
go home?

Why do Hansel and Gretel
think that they would be
welcomed at home?

How does having the witch's
jewels help Hansel and
Gretel?

Do Hansel and Gretel feel
different about themselves
after spending time in the
enchanted forest?

"Now it's time for us to go. We
must get out of this enchanted forest,"
said Hansel. But when they'd walked
for a couple of hours they came to
a wide lake. "We can't get across,"
said Hansel. "There isn't a plank or
a bridge anywhere."

"There isn't a boat either," answered
Gretel, "but there's a little white duck
swimming over there—if I ask her to, she
will help us over." Then she cried:

> "They haven't a bridge and they
>   haven't a plank,
>   **Hansel and Gretel are out of luck.**
>   Please take us across to the
>   other bank
>   **And we'll thank you so, you little**
>   **white duck!"**

The duck did come over to them,
and Hansel sat down on her back and
told his sister to sit behind him.

"No," answered Gretel, "it would be too heavy for the little duck. She can take us over one at a time."

The good little bird did that, and when they were happily on the other side, and had gone on for a little while, they came to a wood that kept looking more and more familiar, and at last, in the distance, they saw their father's house. Then they started to run, burst into the living room, and threw themselves on their father's neck. Since he had left the children in the forest he had not had a single happy hour. His wife, though, had died. Gretel shook out her apron and pearls and precious stones rolled all over the room, and Hansel threw down out of his pocket one handful after another. All their troubles were at an end and they lived together in perfect happiness.

The bravest thing Hansel did was _____

_____

The bravest thing Gretel did was _____

_____

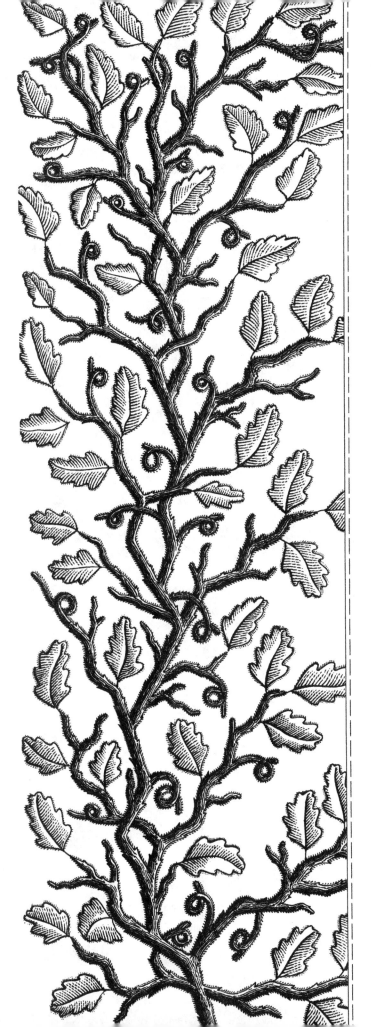

My Question

_____

_____

Name

SPECIAL PLACES

POETRY BY

GWENDOLYN BROOKS

AND

ROBERT FROST,

AND A

NAVAJO POEM

♣

SESSION 1: "Little Puppy"

This session consists of an introduction, two readings of the poem, and an art activity in which children draw what the child and the puppy do during the day.

AT-HOME WORK: "Little Puppy"

The adult partner reads the poem through once, encouraging the child to join in saying the underlined phrases. The adult then reads the poem a second time, pausing to discuss G.B.'s two questions. When called for, children respond to these questions by underlining parts of the poem.

After reading, the adult writes the child's own question about "Little Puppy" into the book.

SESSION 2: "Little Puppy"

During this reading of the poem, you will collect students' responses to G.B.'s questions and lead a discussion of them. The session concludes with an art activity in which students draw what they think is the most enjoyable activity that the child and the puppy do in the late afternoon or evening.

SESSION 3: "Lyle"

This session consists of an introduction and first reading of the poem, a second reading and discussion of the poem, and a writing activity in which children write what they think the tree would say to Lyle.

SESSION 4: "The Pasture"

This session consists of an introduction and first reading of the poem, a second reading and discussion of the poem, and a writing and art activity in which children write "invitation poems" and draw themselves and a companion in their own special place.

SESSION 1: "Little Puppy"

INTRODUCTION

Introduce the poem by telling children that it is about a Navajo child who lives in the southwestern United States. His or her job is to herd sheep—taking them out in the morning to graze and bringing them back in the evening.

FIRST AND SECOND READINGS

Ask children to listen as you read the poem aloud. Before reading the poem a second time, take a few moments to let children ask questions and make comments. Also help children clear up such unfamiliar vocabulary as "cliffs," "fluted," and "hogan," using the definitions given in the margin of your text and referring to the illustrations. Then encourage children to follow along in their books and to join in saying the underlined phrases as you read the poem a second time.

ART ACTIVITY

Tell children that this poem gives a very vivid picture of the land in which the child and the puppy live. Ask students to review the things the child sees when herding the sheep, such as cliffs, red rocks, eagles, the pointed hill, and pools of water. Then have students turn to the page captioned "During the Day" and ask them to draw one of the things the child and the puppy do during the day. Encourage children to include details of the Southwestern landscape in their pictures. Allow time for students to share and compare their drawings.

SESSION 2: "Little Puppy"

POSTING "MY QUESTIONS"

Have students cut out the questions they wrote at home. Glance through them briefly and note any that you might want to raise during your discussion of G.B.'s questions. Then pin students' questions on the Sharing Questions bulletin board. Let children know that even though there will be no Sharing Questions Discussion this week, they should still look at the bulletin board and talk about their questions with each other.

READING AND REVIEW OF G.B.'S QUESTIONS

Read page 64 (the first twelve lines of the poem) aloud, pausing at the end to ask students what things they underlined in that part of the poem. Ask children why they would like to see or do what they have underlined. When appropriate, follow up on their responses by asking additional questions such as those given in the margin of your text.

Read the rest of the poem, collecting students' responses and reasons. Conclude by asking G.B.'s second question and following up on the children's responses.

SESSION 2: "Little Puppy" (continued)

ART ACTIVITY

Remind students that yesterday they drew a picture of what the child and the puppy do in the daytime. Have students turn to the page captioned "When the Sun Goes Down" and tell them to draw what the child does in the late afternoon and evening that they think sounds most enjoyable, such as following the sheep home, looking at the sunset, sitting around the fire, or eating cornbread. Allow time for students to share and compare their drawings.

SESSION 3: "Lyle"

INTRODUCTION

Introduce the session by telling students that this is a poem about a boy named Lyle who has to move with his family from his home.

FIRST READING

Read the poem through while children listen. Afterward, take a few moments to let children ask questions and make comments, and clear up unfamiliar vocabulary.

SECOND READING AND DISCUSSION

Divide the class into three groups and read the poem a second time, having each group read or recite one of the stanzas along with you. When you have finished, help students think further about Lyle's feelings about the tree by asking such questions as *Does Lyle like it that the tree won't go away? Why or why not? Why does Lyle talk about the tree as if it were a person? Why does Lyle think about the tree instead of about his home?*

WRITING ACTIVITY

Make two columns on the board with the headings "Trees don't move" and "People move." Ask students what they think is nice or not nice about trees not being able to move. Then ask them what they think is nice or not nice about people moving from one home to another. Write their answers on the board under the appropriate heading.

Then have students turn to the page with the question "What Would Tree Say to Lyle?" To help students think about their answers, ask such questions as *Would the tree like to move? Would the tree try to comfort Lyle?*

Ask students to write what they think the tree would say, either referring to the columns on the board or making up their own responses. If necessary, help students write their answers in their books.

SESSION 4: "The Pasture"

INTRODUCTION

Introduce the session by telling students that this poem is about life out in the country and that a "pasture" is a field in which cows or other animals are kept so they can eat the grass.

FIRST READING

Ask children to listen as you read the poem aloud. Afterward, take a few moments to let children ask questions and make comments. Also help children clear up such unfamiliar vocabulary as "spring" and "sha'n't," using the definitions given in the margin of your text.

SECOND READING AND DISCUSSION

Read the poem a second time, encouraging students to follow along in their books and to join in saying the last line of each stanza.

After the reading, help students visualize the scene in the poem by asking them to think about how the pasture looks, about what kind of day it might be, and about how the spring looks and sounds when cleared of its dead leaves. Then ask them to consider briefly why they might like to go out to the pasture to see the spring and the newborn calf.

Then, help students think about the person who is speaking in the poem by asking such questions as *Why is the speaker inviting someone else to come too? Why does the speaker think the person would like to come? Why does the speaker promise he or she won't be gone long?*

CREATIVE WRITING AND ART ACTIVITY

Remind children that in both "The Pasture" and "Little Puppy" the speaker is planning to go to a special place and invites someone else to come along. Tell students that they are going to write their own "invitation poems" in which they ask another person or a pet to come with them to their own special place.

Ask students to turn to the page titled "My Invitation." Help them read the beginning of the first line ("Come with me,...") and tell them to finish the line with the name or a description of their companion. Tell students they will complete the second line ("I'm going to...") by writing in the name or a brief description of a special place they like to visit. On the remaining lines, students can add some of the things they expect to see, hear, or do in their special place. Circulate among students, helping them complete their poems.

After students have finished their poems, have them turn to the page captioned "My Special Place." Ask them to draw a picture showing what they and the companion they have invited will do in their special place. Allow time for children to share and compare their drawings.

SPECIAL PLACES

POETRY

Underline what the child sees or does during the day that you would enjoy.

LITTLE PUPPY

Little puppy with the black spots,

Come and herd the flock with me.

We will climb the red rocks

And from the top we'll see

The tall cliffs, the straight cliffs,

The fluted cliffs,

Where the eagles live.

We'll see the dark rocks,

The smooth rocks,

That hold the rain to give us

Water, when we eat our bread and meat,

When the sun is high.

cliffs: steep, rocky sides of a mountain, hill, or canyon

fluted: having grooves

Why is it fun to climb rocks?

Why would it be fun to see eagles?

Why is it fun to eat outside or drink water from the rocks?

Little spotted dog of mine,

Come and spend the day with me,

When the sun is going down

Behind the pointed hill,

We will follow home the flock.

They will lead the way

To the hogans where the fires burn

And the square cornbread is in the ashes,

Waiting our return.

hogan: a type of Navajo house made of logs and mud

—Navajo poem

Why is it nice to go home after spending a day outside?

Why is it fun to eat around a fire?

Why will the child enjoy his or her day?

Why does the child think the day will be more fun if the puppy comes along?

Why are things nicer when they are shared?

Why might the child in the poem particularly want to have a companion?

During the Day

When the Sun Goes Down

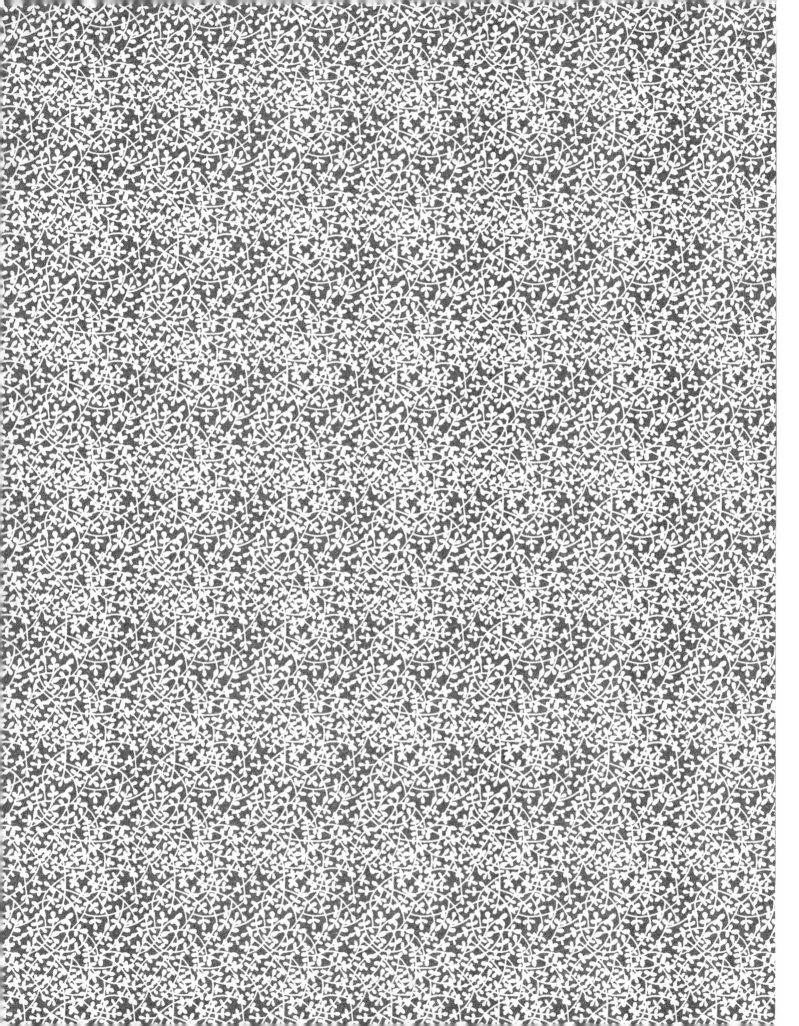

My Question

_____

_____

_____

Name _____

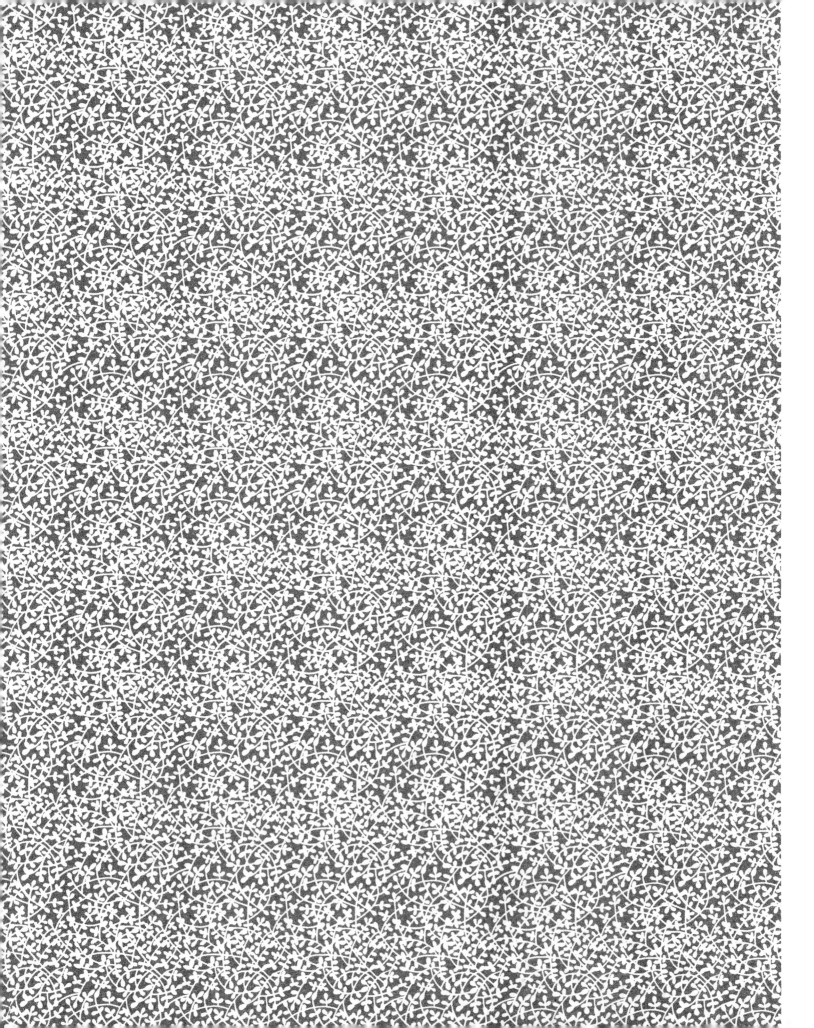

LYLE

Tree won't pack his bag and go.
Tree won't go away.
In his first and favorite home
Tree shall stay and stay.

Once I liked a little home.
Then I liked another.
I've waved Good-bye to seven homes.
And so have Pops and Mother.

But tree may stay, so stout and straight.
And never have to move,
As I, as Pops, as Mother,
From land he learned to love.

—Gwendolyn Brooks

71

What Would Tree Say to Lyle?

_____

_____

_____

_____

_____

THE PASTURE

I'm going out to clean the pasture spring;
I'll only stop to rake the leaves away
(And wait to watch the water clear, I may):
I sha'n't be gone long. —You come too.

I'm going out to fetch the little calf
That's standing by the mother. It's so young
It totters when she licks it with her tongue.
I sha'n't be gone long. —You come too.

—Robert Frost

pasture: a field in which animals are kept so they can eat the grass

spring: water that flows up out of the ground to make a brook

sha'n't: shall not

My Invitation

Come with me, _____

I'm going to _____

I will _____

I will _____

And I will _____

_____

You come too.

74

My Special Place

MOTHER OF THE WATERS

HAITIAN FOLKTALE
AS TOLD BY
DIANE WOLKSTEIN

OVERVIEW

SESSION 1

This session consists of an introduction and first reading of the story, followed by a brief sharing of questions and comments, and an art activity in which children draw their interpretation of the Mother of the Waters.

AT-HOME WORK

During this second reading, the adult partner encourages the child to join in saying the underlined words and phrases, and pauses to discuss G.B.'s two questions. Children respond to these questions by underlining parts of the story.

After reading, the adult writes the child's own question about the story into the book in preparation for the Sharing Questions Discussion (Session 4).

SESSION 2

During this reading of the story, you will collect students' responses to G.B.'s questions and lead a discussion of them. The session concludes with a drawing activity in which children illustrate how they think the first girl's life changes as a result of her stay with the Mother of the Waters.

SESSION 3

This session consists of a dramatization in which children compare how the two girls respond to the Mother of the Waters' tests.

SESSION 4

This session consists of a Sharing Questions Discussion and an evaluative discussion in which students consider whether they like or dislike the way the Mother of the Waters treats the girls.

SESSION 1

INTRODUCTION

Begin the session by telling children that this story comes from Haiti, a country in the Caribbean.

FIRST READING AND SHARING OF RESPONSES

Ask children to listen as you read the story aloud. As you come to the words "thistle" and "crossroads," explain them briefly, using the definitions given in the margin of your text.

After the reading, allow a few moments to clear up unfamiliar vocabulary and to let students ask questions and share their initial reactions to the story. Encourage children to offer their opinions about which parts of the story they especially liked and why.

ART ACTIVITY

Have children create the frontispiece for the story by drawing what they think the Mother of the Waters looks like. Briefly review what they know about her. Allow time for students to share and compare their illustrations.

SESSION 2

POSTING "MY QUESTIONS"

Have students cut out the questions they wrote at home and pin them on the Sharing Questions bulletin board. Children who have not had an at-home reading can dictate their questions to you at this time. Encourage children to look at the Sharing Questions bulletin board during the week, to point out their own questions and to ask about those of their classmates.

READING AND REVIEW OF G.B.'S QUESTIONS

Read the story aloud, encouraging children to follow along in their books. Pause to collect students' responses to G.B.'s questions (pages 10 and 14). Help students think further about the two girls and the spirit in which each fulfills the Mother of the Waters' tasks, by asking additional questions such as those given in the margin of your text.

SESSION 2 (continued)

ART ACTIVITY

Introduce the activity by telling students that they are going to think about how things will be different for the first girl as a result of her stay with the Mother of the Waters. Help them develop their ideas by asking such questions as *What has the first girl learned from the Mother of the Waters? How will she use her silverware? What kind of life will she have when she grows up?*

Then have students turn to the page captioned "When the first girl grows up she will...." Ask them to draw a picture showing how the first girl lives after her stay with the Mother of the Waters. As children draw, circulate among them and help them complete their captions. Allow time for students to share and compare their drawings.

SESSION 3

PREPARING CHILDREN FOR DRAMATIZATION

Remind children that the Mother of the Waters asks the two girls to do certain things for her so that she can find out what kind of people they are. Tell students that now they are going to act out these tests. Briefly review the tests: washing the old woman's back; cooking dinner from a bean, a grain of rice, and a bone; responding to the begging cat; and choosing an egg.

Before each scene, prepare actors and audience by asking such questions as *Why does the Mother of the Waters ask the girls to do this particular thing? What is she trying to find out about the girls?*

DRAMATIZATION

Divide the class into groups of three and assign the roles of the Mother of the Waters, the first girl, and the second girl.

Have children act out each test twice, once with the first girl and once with the second, so that they can compare the actions and words of the two girls.

Conclude the session by asking the class, *What has each girl shown about herself?* Try to help students get beyond simply describing the girls as "good" or "bad." Encourage them to name specific qualities that the old woman is seeking and that the girls show or don't show during the tests, such as kindness or politeness.

SESSION 4

SHARING QUESTIONS DISCUSSION

Prepare for discussion as usual, deciding on the five or six interpretive questions you intend to ask the class. Note which of the children's questions are similar to those you plan to lead and try to include three or four of their questions in your final list. When you write your questions on the board, include children's names as appropriate.

Suggested Interpretive Questions

What does the Mother of the Waters want the girls to learn?

Why does the old woman set up her tests so that some require obedience and others require disobedience?

Why does the Mother of the Waters give both girls the same chances even though the first girl is kinder than the second?

Does the Mother of the Waters care about what happens to the girls?

EVALUATIVE DISCUSSION

Introduce the activity by telling children that sometimes we have different opinions about characters in stories, depending on what we ourselves like or dislike about people.

Write on the board the following question and headings:

Do you like the way the Mother of the Waters treats the girls?

Yes   No

As children offer their opinions, ask for their reasons and write a word or two for each under the appropriate heading. Children may give reasons on both sides if they like.

After the class has debated the question for five or ten minutes, ask children to turn to the page at the end of the story on which the question is printed. Reread the question and ask them to circle either "yes" or "no" for their answer. Review the reasons on the board and ask children to copy the ones they like best on the lines provided.

MOTHER OF THE WATERS

HAITIAN FOLKTALE

Mother of the Waters

There was once a young girl whose
mother and father were both dead.
As she had no way to get anything to eat,
she had to hire herself out as a
servant. She worked for a woman who
lived by the river. But even though
the woman had a daughter the same age
as the servant girl, she showed no
kindness to her. She beat her and spoke
roughly to her and gave her only
scraps to eat.

One day, the woman sent the
servant girl to the river to wash
the silverware. As the girl was washing

the silver, a tiny silver teaspoon slipped through her fingers and was carried away by the water. The servant girl reached for the teaspoon, but the current was moving too swiftly. She went back to the house and told her mistress what had happened.

"Find my teaspoon," the woman screamed, "or never return to my house."

The servant girl returned to the river and followed the stream. She walked all day without finding the teaspoon, and as the sun began to set in the sky, she started crying.

An old woman sitting on a stone near the river's edge asked her why she was crying.

"I have dropped my mistress's silver teaspoon in the river. She says if I do not find it, I may not return. I will have no work. How will I eat?"

The old woman did not answer.
Instead, she asked, "Will you wash
my back?"

"Of course," the girl answered.

She soaped and scrubbed the
old woman's back, but the woman's back
was rough and hard and covered
with sores and thistles, and the girl's
hands were soon bleeding.

thistle: a weed
with sharp prickles

"What is it?" the woman asked.

"It is nothing," the girl answered.

"Let me see your hands," the
old woman said.

The girl held them out. The old
woman spit on them. The cuts closed
up and the girl's hands were as they
were before.

"Come home with me," the
old woman said, "and I will give you
dinner."

On these two pages, underline some things the first girl does that please the Mother of the Waters.

Why does the Mother of the Waters tell the first girl to beat the cat?

Why is she pleased that the first girl did not beat the cat?

She led the girl to her home in the mountains and gave her banana pudding. Then they went to sleep.

The next day, after the girl had swept the yard, the woman gave her a bone, a grain of rice, and one bean and told her to make dinner.

"Grandmother," the girl said respectfully, "please forgive me, but I do not know how to make dinner with these."

"It is simple," the old woman said. "Place them in a pot of boiling water and dinner will soon be ready."

The girl followed the woman's directions, and by noon a delicious-smelling casserole of rice, beans, and meat was steaming inside the pot.

As they ate the old woman told the girl: "I will be going out. In a few hours a wild cat will come and beg for food. Do not give it any food. Beat it with my stick."

10

A few hours after the old woman
left, the girl heard a mewing outside the
door. *Me-ow. Me-ow. Me-ow.* The cat
was so thin and hungry the girl did
not have the heart to hit it. She brought
it a saucer of milk and watched it
eat. After a while the cat went away.

A short time later the old woman
returned. She was pleased with the girl.
So the servant girl stayed on with
the old woman. The girl helped her,
and the old woman always gave her
enough to eat.

Then, after several months,
the old woman told her it was time for
her to return to her mistress.

"Yes," said the girl. "But how can I go
back without the silver teaspoon?"

crossroads: a place where two roads meet; an intersection

"Walk down the road," the old woman said. "When you come to the first crossroads you will see a pile of eggs lying on some straw. The larger ones will call out: *Take me, take me!* Take one of the smaller eggs and break it open at the next crossroads."

The servant girl thanked the old woman and set out.

At the first crossroads she saw the pile of eggs. The larger ones cried: *Take me, take me!* The girl chose the smallest egg and when she cracked it open at the next crossroads, out came a tiny box, which grew and grew until it filled her arms. The girl opened it and inside were forks and knives and spoons—all made of silver.

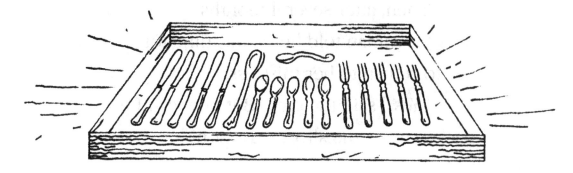

The woman and her daughter
were so jealous when they saw the servant
girl's box of silverware that they made
her tell the story of how she had gotten it
three times. Then the very next morning,
the mother sent her own daughter
down to the river to wash the silverware.

The girl didn't even bother
to wash the silverware. She simply threw
the small coffee teaspoon into the
river and went home.

"I have lost the coffee spoon,"
the girl declared.

"Then go and find it," the mother
said knowingly, "and do not come
home until you do."

The daughter walked alongside
the river all day. Then, toward evening,
she saw the old woman sitting on
a stone. Immediately she began to cry.

"Why are you crying?" the woman
asked.

On these two pages, underline some things the second girl does that show she cannot learn.

Why does beating the cat, as she was told to do, show that the second girl cannot learn?

Why does the Mother of the Waters come back hurt after the second girl beats the cat?

"Oh-oh. I have lost my mother's silver spoon. She says I may not go home unless I find it. What shall I do?"

"Will you wash my back?" the woman asked.

The girl took the soap and began to wash the woman's back when the thistles on the woman's back cut her hands.

"Oh-oh!" she cried.

"What is it?" asked the woman.

"It's your filthy rotting back. It cut my hands and they are bleeding."

The old woman took the girl's hands and spit on them and they were healed. Then she brought her to her home in the mountains and fed her supper.

The next morning, the old woman
gave the girl a bone, a grain of rice,
and one bean and told her to make
dinner.

"With this garbage?" said the girl.

"What a sorry tongue you have,"
the woman answered. "I only hope you
are not as nasty as your words.
Place what I have given you in a pot
of boiling water and dinner will soon
be ready."

At noon the pot was filled with
rice and beans and meat. They ate their
meal and the old woman said:

"I am going out. In a few hours
a wild cat will come and beg for
food. Do not give it any food. Beat it
with my stick."

Some time after the old woman left, the girl heard a mewing outside. *Me-ow. Me-ow. Me-ow.* She grabbed the old woman's stick and rushed for the cat. She hit it and hit it and hit it and hit it until she broke one of its legs.

Much later that evening, the old woman returned. She was leaning on a cane and limping, for one of her legs was broken. The next morning she told the girl: "You must leave my house today. You will not learn and I cannot help you anymore."

"But I will not go home without my silverware," the girl insisted.

"Then I shall give you one last bit of advice. At the next crossroads you will find a pile of eggs lying on some straw. The larger ones will call out: *Take me, take me!* Choose one of the smaller eggs and break it open at the next crossroads."

The girl ran out of the house
and down the road. When she came to
the first crossroads the larger eggs
called out: ***Take me, take me!***

"I am not foolish," said the
girl. "If an egg speaks to me, I will listen.
If it is a large one, all the better!"

She chose the largest egg and
broke it open at the next crossroads.
Out came all kinds of lizards, goblins,
demons, and devils and ate the girl up.

When the first girl grows up she will _____

_____

Do you like the way the Mother of the Waters treats the girls?

YES   NO

Why or why not? _____

_____

_____

_____

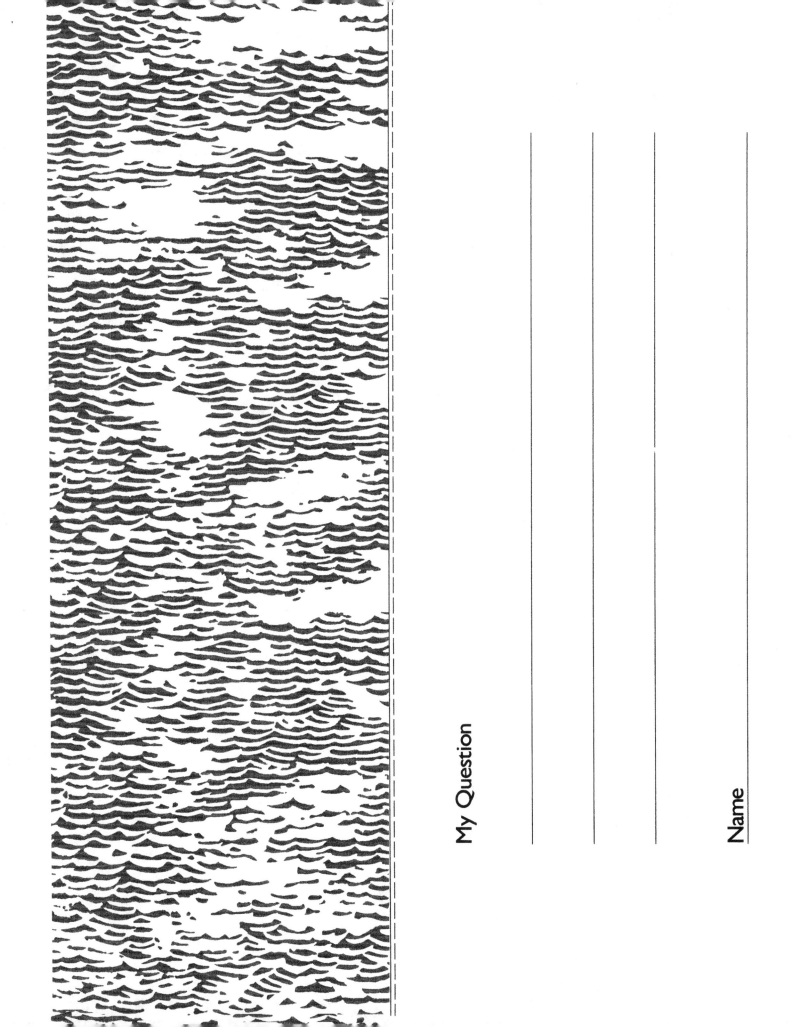

My Question

Name

ZLATEH
THE GOAT

ISAAC BASHEVIS SINGER

SESSION 1

This session consists of an introduction and first reading of the story, followed by a brief sharing of questions and comments, and an art activity in which children draw an anthropomorphic portrait of Zlateh.

AT-HOME WORK

During this second reading, the adult partner encourages the child to join in saying the underlined words, and pauses to discuss G.B.'s three questions. Children respond to these questions by underlining parts of the story.

After reading, the adult writes the child's own question about the story into the book.

SESSION 2

During this reading of the story, you will collect students' responses to G.B.'s questions and lead a discussion of them. The session concludes with an art activity in which children create a "mood drawing" of what they think it felt like during the blizzard.

SESSION 3

This session consists of a textual analysis, an interpretive discussion, and an art activity in which children create a mood drawing of the night after the blizzard.

SESSION 4

This session consists of a dramatization in which children act out situations without using words, communicating non-verbally as Aaron and Zlateh do in the story. Prepare for this session by writing a number of scenarios on notecards that children can then draw out of a container. See the directions in Session 4 for suggested scenarios.

SESSION 1

INTRODUCTION

Begin the session by telling children that the story takes place among Jewish people living in Poland in the early 1900's. Hanukkah is a Jewish holiday that people celebrate by lighting candles and eating foods cooked in oil.

FIRST READING AND SHARING OF RESPONSES

Ask children to listen as you read the story aloud. As you come to the words "furrier" and "dreidel," explain them briefly, using the definitions given in the margin of your text.

After the reading, allow a few moments to clear up unfamiliar vocabulary and to let students ask questions and share their initial reactions to the story. Encourage children to offer their opinions about which parts of the story they especially liked and why.

ART ACTIVITY

Have children turn to the frontispiece, captioned "How I Imagine Zlateh," and ask them to draw what they think Zlateh would look like if she were a human being. Help them imagine their pictures by asking such questions as *Do you imagine Zlateh as a patient and wise old person? Do you think that because she feeds Aaron, she is like a mother? Do you think that because Aaron leads her to safety and takes care of her, she is like a little girl, or do you think she and Aaron are exactly the same age because they understand and help each other?*

Allow time for students to share and compare their illustrations.

SESSION 2

POSTING "MY QUESTIONS"

Have students cut out the questions they wrote at home. Glance through them briefly and note any that you might want to raise during your discussion of G.B.'s questions. Then pin students' questions on the Sharing Questions bulletin board. Let children know that even though there will be no Sharing Questions Discussion this week, they should still look at the bulletin board and talk about their questions with each other.

READING AND REVIEW OF G.B.'S QUESTIONS

Read the story aloud, encouraging children to follow along in their books. Pause to collect students' responses to G.B.'s questions (pages 28, 32, and 36). Help students think further about why they underlined their particular passages by asking additional questions such as those given in the margin of your text.

SESSION 2 (continued)

ART ACTIVITY

Have students turn to the facing pages captioned "The Blizzard" and "After the Blizzard." Introduce the activity by telling them that they are going to create mood drawings for each of the two very different experiences of snow in the story. Read aloud the passage describing the blizzard on page 31 beginning, "The snow grew thicker," and ending, "A white dust rose above the ground." Ask the class to think about the question *How would the blizzard make you feel if you were there?*

After students have offered a few ideas, tell them that now they are going to draw a picture showing what they think it felt like during the blizzard. Make sure they understand that this is an opportunity to show how the description made them *feel*, both physically and emotionally, by using colors, shapes, or things they associate with those feelings.

You might also suggest that children draw imaginary things that fit the mood of the storm. For example, the author said the snowstorm looked "as if white imps were playing tag on the fields."

Let students know that they will draw the second picture, "After the Blizzard," during their next Read-Aloud session.

SESSION 3

TEXTUAL ANALYSIS

Read aloud the passage on page 38 beginning, "The snow fell for three days," and ending on page 39, "The moon swam in the sky as in a sea." Help students reflect upon Aaron's thoughts in this section of the story by conducting a textual analysis, asking questions such as those given in your text.

INTERPRETIVE DISCUSSION

At the end of your textual analysis, lead a discussion of the following interpretive question:

> *Why does Aaron decide in the haystack that he will never part with Zlateh?*

ART ACTIVITY

Have children create their "After the Blizzard" mood drawings following the procedure described in Session 2. Encourage students to think about the feelings they might have after a three-day snowstorm (for example, relief, gratitude, hope, or joy) and to use colors, shapes, and images that reflect those feelings.

S E S S I O N 4

PREPARING CHILDREN FOR DRAMATIZATION

Remind children that in the story the characters can understand Zlateh even though she cannot talk. Ask students to offer examples of ways animals can show their thoughts and feelings. Then ask them to think of ways *people* can communicate without using words (for instance, hand gestures and facial expressions).

Tell students that now they will have a chance to act out some situations, without using words, while their classmates try to guess what the situations are.

DRAMATIZATION

Divide the class into groups of four so that one pair of students can act out a situation while the second pair watches their performance and guesses. Place in a container the notecards on which you have written the situations to be dramatized. Have each pair of students draw from the container and perform the scene they select.

Suggested Situations

1. Person A is sad.
   Person B tries to comfort Person A.

2. Person A wants to play with Person B.
   Person B would like to play but can't.

3. Person A has won a prize.
   Person B congratulates Person A.

4. Person A tells Person B a secret.
   Person B is surprised.

5. Person A is new in school.
   Person B makes friends with Person A.

6. Person A and Person B meet after being apart a long time.

7. Person A teases Person B.
   Person B pretends not to care.

8. Person A is afraid to try something new.
   Person B encourages Person A to try.

9. Person A is angry.
   Person B tries to calm Person A down.

10. Person A's feelings have been hurt.
    Person B tries to make Person A laugh.

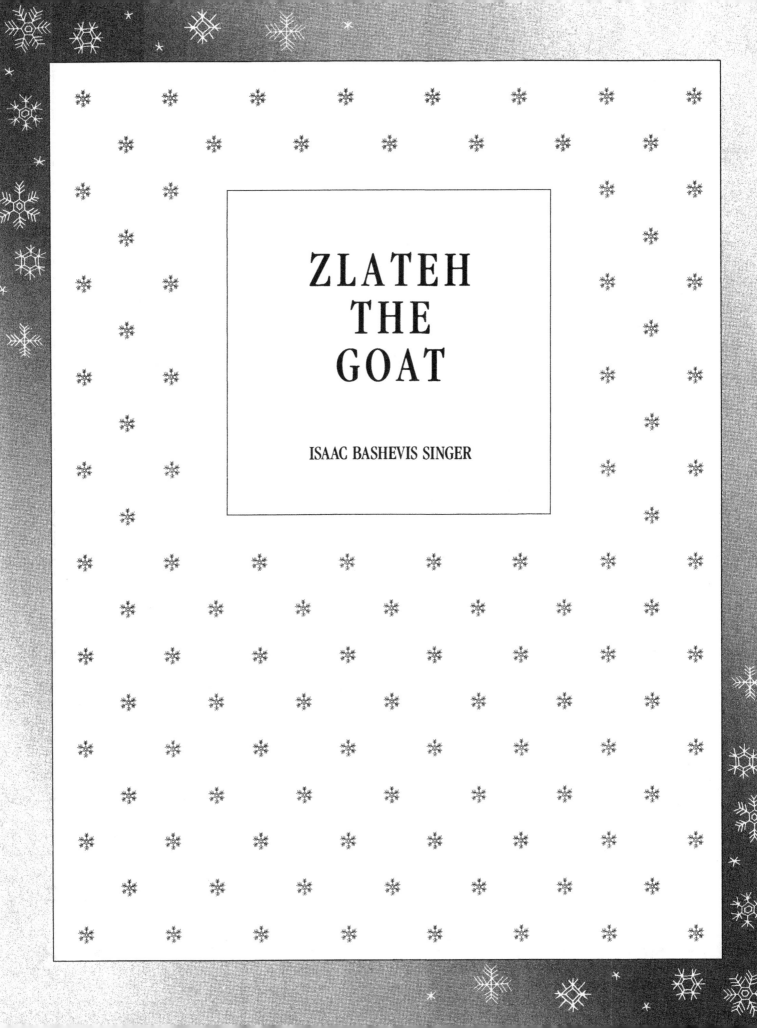

ZLATEH THE GOAT

ISAAC BASHEVIS SINGER

How I Imagine Zlateh

At Hanukkah time the road from
the village to the town is usually
covered with snow, but this year the
winter had been a mild one. Hanukkah
had almost come, yet little snow
had fallen. The sun shone most of the
time. The peasants complained that
because of the dry weather there would
be a poor harvest of winter grain.
New grass sprouted, and the peasants
sent their cattle out to pasture.

For Reuven the furrier it was
a bad year, and after long hesitation he
decided to sell Zlateh the goat. She was
old and gave little milk. Feivel the town
butcher had offered eight gulden for her.

furrier: a person
who makes and sells
clothing made out
of fur

25

Such a sum would buy Hanukkah candles, potatoes and oil for pancakes, gifts for the children, and other holiday necessaries for the house. Reuven told his oldest boy Aaron to take the goat to town.

Aaron understood what taking the goat to Feivel meant, but had to obey his father. Leah, his mother, wiped the tears from her eyes when she heard the news. Aaron's younger sisters, Anna and Miriam, cried loudly. Aaron put on his quilted jacket and a cap with earmuffs, bound a rope around Zlateh's neck, and took along two slices of bread with cheese to eat on the road.

Aaron was supposed to deliver the
goat by evening, spend the night at the
butcher's, and return the next day
with the money.

While the family said goodbye
to the goat, and Aaron placed the rope
around her neck, Zlateh stood as
patiently and good-naturedly as ever.
She licked Reuven's hand. She shook her
small white beard. Zlateh trusted
human beings. She knew that they always
fed her and never did her any harm.

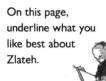

On this page, underline what you like best about Zlateh.

Do you like Zlateh for trusting people? Why or why not?

Do you like Zlateh for deciding that "a goat shouldn't ask questions"? Why or why not?

When Aaron brought her out on the road to town, she seemed somewhat astonished. She'd never been led in that direction before. She looked back at him questioningly, as if to say, "Where are you taking me?" But after a while she seemed to come to the conclusion that a goat shouldn't ask questions. Still, the road was different. They passed new fields, pastures, and huts with thatched roofs. Here and there a dog barked and came running after them, but Aaron chased it away with his stick.

28

The sun was shining when Aaron
left the village. Suddenly the weather
changed. A large black cloud with
a bluish center appeared in the east and
spread itself rapidly over the sky.
A cold wind blew in with it. The crows
flew low, croaking. At first it looked
as if it would rain, but instead it began
to hail as in summer. It was early
in the day, but it became dark as dusk.
After a while the hail turned to snow.

In his twelve years Aaron had seen
all kinds of weather, but he had never
experienced a snow like this one. It was
so dense it shut out the light of the day.
In a short time their path was completely
covered. The wind became as cold
as ice. The road to town was narrow

and winding. Aaron no longer knew
where he was. He could not see through
the snow. The cold soon penetrated
his quilted jacket.

At first Zlateh didn't seem to
mind the change in weather. She, too,
was twelve years old and knew
what winter meant. But when her legs
sank deeper and deeper into the snow,
she began to turn her head and look at
Aaron in wonderment. Her mild eyes
seemed to ask, "Why are we out in such
a storm?" Aaron hoped that a peasant
would come along with his cart, but no
one passed by.

The snow grew thicker, falling
to the ground in large, whirling flakes.
Beneath it Aaron's boots touched
the softness of a plowed field. He realized
that he was no longer on the road.
He had gone astray. He could no longer
figure out which was east or west,
which way was the village, the town.
The wind whistled, howled, whirled the
snow about in eddies. It looked as if white
imps were playing tag on the fields.
A white dust rose above the ground.
Zlateh stopped. She could walk no
longer. Stubbornly she anchored her
cleft hooves in the earth and bleated as
if pleading to be taken home. Icicles hung
from her white beard, and her horns
were glazed with frost.

On these two pages, underline what you like best about Aaron.

Why doesn't Aaron want to admit the danger?

Why do you like Aaron for including Zlateh in his prayers?

Why does Aaron take such good care of Zlateh?

Aaron did not want to admit the danger, but he knew just the same that if they did not find shelter they would freeze to death. This was no ordinary storm. It was a mighty blizzard. The snowfall had reached his knees. His hands were numb, and he could no longer feel his toes. He choked when he breathed. His nose felt like wood, and he rubbed it with snow. Zlateh's bleating began to sound like crying. Those humans in whom she had so much confidence had dragged her into a trap. Aaron began to pray to God for himself and for the innocent animal.

Suddenly he made out the shape of a hill. He wondered what it could be. Who had piled snow into such a huge heap? He moved toward it, dragging Zlateh after him. When he came near it, he realized that it was a large haystack which the snow had blanketed.

Aaron realized immediately that
they were saved. With great effort
he dug his way through the snow.
He was a village boy and knew what
to do. When he reached the hay,
he hollowed out a nest for himself and
the goat. No matter how cold it may
be outside, in the hay it is always warm.
And hay was food for Zlateh. The
moment she smelled it she became
contented and began to eat. Outside,
the snow continued to fall. It quickly
covered the passageway Aaron had dug.
But a boy and an animal need to
breathe, and there was hardly any air
in their hideout. Aaron bored a kind of
a window through the hay and snow
and carefully kept the passage clear.

Zlateh, having eaten her fill, sat down on her hind legs and seemed to have regained her confidence in man. Aaron ate his two slices of bread and cheese, but after the difficult journey he was still hungry. He looked at Zlateh and noticed her udders were full. He lay down next to her, placing himself so that when he milked her he could squirt the milk into his mouth. It was rich and sweet. Zlateh was not accustomed to being milked that way, but she did not resist. On the contrary, she seemed eager to reward Aaron for bringing her to a shelter whose very walls, floor, and ceiling were made of food.

Through the window Aaron could catch a glimpse of the chaos outside. The wind carried before it whole drifts of snow. It was completely dark, and he did not know whether night had already come or whether it was

the darkness of the storm. Thank God
that in the hay it was not cold. The dried
hay, grass, and field flowers exuded
the warmth of the summer sun.
Zlateh ate frequently; she nibbled from
above, below, from the left and right.
Her body gave forth an animal warmth,
and Aaron cuddled up to her. He had
always loved Zlateh, but now she was like a
sister. He was alone, cut off from his family,
and wanted to talk. He began to talk
to Zlateh. "Zlateh, what do you think about
what has happened to us?" he asked.

"**Maaaa**," Zlateh answered.

"If we hadn't found this stack of hay,
we would both be frozen stiff by now,"
Aaron said.

"**Maaaa**," was the goat's reply.

"If the snow keeps on falling like this,
we may have to stay here for days,"
Aaron explained.

"**Maaaa**," Zlateh bleated.

On these two pages, underline what you think Zlateh likes best about Aaron.

Why does Aaron tell Zlateh stories?

How can Aaron understand what Zlateh is saying?

Why is Aaron comforted by Zlateh's patience?

"What does 'maaaa' mean?" Aaron asked. "You'd better speak up clearly."

"**Maaaa, maaaa,**" Zlateh tried.

"Well, let it be 'maaaa' then," Aaron said patiently. "You can't speak, but I know you understand. I need you and you need me. Isn't that right?"

"**Maaaa.**"

Aaron became sleepy. He made a pillow out of some hay, leaned his head on it, and dozed off. Zlateh, too, fell asleep.

When Aaron opened his eyes, he didn't know whether it was morning or night. The snow had blocked up his window. He tried to clear it, but when he had bored through to the length of his arm, he still hadn't reached the outside. Luckily he had his stick with him and was able to break through to the open air. It was still dark outside. The snow continued to fall and the wind wailed, first with one voice and then

36

with many. Sometimes it had the sound of devilish laughter. Zlateh, too, awoke, and when Aaron greeted her, she answered, "**Maaaa**." Yes, Zlateh's language consisted of only one word, but it meant many things. Now she was saying, "We must accept all that God gives us—heat, cold, hunger, satisfaction, light, and darkness."

Aaron had awakened hungry. He had eaten up his food, but Zlateh had plenty of milk.

For three days Aaron and Zlateh stayed in the haystack. Aaron had always loved Zlateh, but in these three days he loved her more and more. She fed him with her milk and helped him keep warm. She comforted him with her patience. He told her many stories, and she always cocked her ears and listened. When he patted her, she licked his hand and his face. Then she said, "**Maaaa**," and he knew it meant, I love you, too.

The snow fell for three days, though after the first day it was not as thick and the wind quieted down. Sometimes Aaron felt that there could never have been a summer, that the snow had always fallen, ever since he could remember. He, Aaron, never had a father or mother or sisters. He was a snow child, born of the snow, and so was Zlateh. It was so quiet in the hay that his ears rang in the stillness. Aaron and Zlateh slept all night and a good part of the day. As for Aaron's dreams, they were all about warm weather. He dreamed of green fields, trees covered with blossoms, clear brooks, and singing birds.

Textual Analysis Questions

Why does Aaron feel as if he never had a father or mother or sisters?

Why does Aaron think of himself and Zlateh as snow children, born of the snow?

Why does Aaron have only happy dreams?

Why does the world outside the haystack look so beautiful to Aaron, even though he doesn't want to go outside yet?

By the third night the snow had stopped,
but Aaron did not dare to find his
way home in the darkness. The sky
became clear and the moon shone,
casting silvery nets on the snow.
Aaron dug his way out and looked at
the world. It was all white, quiet,
dreaming dreams of heavenly splendor.
The stars were large and close.
The moon swam in the sky as in a sea.

On the morning of the fourth day
Aaron heard the ringing of sleigh bells.
The haystack was not far from the road.
The peasant who drove the sleigh

pointed out the way to him—not to the town and Feivel the butcher, but home to the village. Aaron had decided in the haystack that he would never part with Zlateh.

Aaron's family and their neighbors had searched for the boy and the goat but had found no trace of them during the storm. They feared they were lost. Aaron's mother and sisters cried for him; his father remained silent and gloomy. Suddenly one of the neighbors came running to their house with the news that Aaron and Zlateh were coming up the road.

There was great joy in the family.
Aaron told them how he had found
the stack of hay and how Zlateh had fed
him with her milk. Aaron's sisters
kissed and hugged Zlateh and gave her
a special treat of chopped carrots and
potato peels, which Zlateh gobbled
up hungrily.

Nobody ever again thought
of selling Zlateh, and now that the cold
weather had finally set in, the villagers
needed the services of Reuven the
furrier once more. When Hanukkah came,
Aaron's mother was able to fry
pancakes every evening, and Zlateh

got her portion, too. Even though Zlateh had her own pen, she often came to the kitchen, knocking on the door with her horns to indicate that she was ready to visit, and she was always admitted. In the evening Aaron, Miriam, and Anna played dreidel. Zlateh sat near the stove watching the children and the flickering of the Hanukkah candles.

dreidel: a top used to play a special Hanukkah game

Once in a while Aaron would ask her, "Zlateh, do you remember the three days we spent together?"

And Zlateh would scratch her neck with a horn, shake her white bearded head, and come out with the single sound which expressed all her thoughts, and all her love.

The Blizzard

After the Blizzard

My Question

Name

SECRET MESSAGES

POETRY BY
ROBERT LOUIS STEVENSON,
BARBARA JUSTER ESBENSEN,
AND
EMILY DICKINSON

OVERVIEW

SESSION 1: "The Dumb Soldier"

This session consists of an introduction, two readings of the poem, and an art activity in which children draw their interpretation of the "fairy things" the soldier sees in the grass.

AT-HOME WORK: "The Dumb Soldier"

The adult partner reads the poem through once, encouraging the child to join in saying the underlined phrases. The adult then reads the poem a second time, pausing to discuss G.B.'s two questions.

After reading, the adult writes the child's own question about "The Dumb Soldier" into the book in preparation for the Sharing Questions Discussion (Session 2).

SESSION 2: "The Dumb Soldier"

During this reading of the poem, you will collect students' responses to G.B.'s questions and lead a brief discussion of them. The session concludes with a Sharing Questions Discussion and an art activity in which students draw a world they would like to experience.

SESSION 3: "Snow Print Two: Hieroglyphics"

This session consists of an introduction and first reading of the poem, a second reading and discussion of the poem, and a group writing and art activity in which children compose their own bird secrets in picture writing.

SESSION 4: "Bee! I'm Expecting You!"

This session consists of an introduction and first reading of the poem, a second reading and discussion of the poem, and a group writing and art activity in which children compose the bee's reply to the fly and draw a picture of the bee and the fly together.

SESSION 1: "The Dumb Soldier"

INTRODUCTION

Introduce the poem by explaining to children that it is about a boy who plays with his toy soldier. The soldier is called "dumb" because it cannot speak, and it is made of *lead,* a heavy kind of metal. A *grenadier* is a special kind of soldier.

FIRST AND SECOND READINGS

Ask children to listen as you read the poem aloud. Before reading the poem a second time, take a few moments to let children ask questions and make comments. Also help children clear up such unfamiliar vocabulary as "apace," "scythe is stoned," and "disclose," using the definitions given in the margin of your text.

Then encourage children to follow along in their books as you read the poem aloud a second time. Ask them to join in chorusing the fifth stanza—the turning point of the poem—and the last stanza.

ART ACTIVITY

Have students turn to the page captioned "What the Soldier Sees" and tell them that they will have a chance to imagine what kinds of "fairy things" the toy soldier sees in the "forests of the grass." Help them get ideas for their drawings by asking such questions as *What games might you play among tall grass and spring flowers? If you were so tiny that grass seemed like trees, what creatures might you meet? What kind of magic would you find?* Allow time for children to share and compare their illustrations.

SESSION 2: "The Dumb Soldier"

POSTING "MY QUESTIONS"

Have students cut out the questions they wrote at home. Glance through them briefly and note any you would like to include in the Sharing Questions Discussion before pinning them on the Sharing Questions bulletin board.

READING AND REVIEW OF G.B.'S QUESTIONS

Read the poem aloud, pausing after the fifth stanza and the last stanza to collect responses to G.B.'s questions. Encourage students to give reasons for their answers and then help them think further about the poem by asking additional questions such as those printed in the margin of your text.

SHARING QUESTIONS DISCUSSION

Move directly from your review of G.B.'s second question into the Sharing Questions Discussion. When you write your questions on the board, note which of your questions are similar to the children's and include their names as appropriate.

Suggested Interpretive Questions

Why does the boy think his soldier can see "fairy things" in the grass?

Why does the boy choose a soldier instead of another toy?

Why does the boy imagine that the soldier can see but not speak?

Why does the boy want to make up the soldier's tale himself?

SESSION 2: "The Dumb Soldier" (continued)

ART ACTIVITY

Remind children that the boy in the poem says he would like to live in the grass, like his toy soldier. Ask students to think about places in the world they would like to see but can't because they are people. Would they like to live in the ocean and play with seals and whales? Or fly among the birds? What would they see, hear, and learn there?

Have students turn to the page captioned "I would like to see..." and ask them to draw that place. As children work, circulate among them and help them complete their captions. Allow time for students to share and compare their drawings.

SESSION 3: "Snow Print Two: Hieroglyphics"

INTRODUCTION

Tell students that "hieroglyphics" is a special kind of writing that uses pictures instead of letters. In this poem, the hieroglyphics are the marks the birds make on the snow with their feet.

FIRST READING

Read the poem through while children listen. Before reading the poem a second time, take a few moments to let children ask questions and make comments, and clear up unfamiliar vocabulary.

SECOND READING AND DISCUSSION

As you read the poem a second time, encourage students to follow along in their books. When you have finished, help students think further about the communication between the birds and the person speaking in the poem by asking such questions as *Why is the person in the poem able to "read" the birds' secret messages? Why does the person think the messages are for him or her? How do you think the speaker feels about the birds' messages? Why do the birds' footprints make the speaker think of lost songs and cold wind?*

GROUP CREATIVE WRITING AND ART ACTIVITY

Ask students to think of other "scribbled secrets" the birds might have. Label a section of the board "Bird Secrets" and collect several examples from the class.

Tell children that they are going to write their own bird secrets in picture writing. As an example to help them get started, write on another section of the board "the howling wind that claws like a cat." Have the class briefly suggest some ways this phrase could be written in pictures. (You might ask a few volunteers to draw examples on the board.)

Then ask students to turn to the page titled "Messages From a Bird." Have them look back over the list of "Bird Secrets" on the board and write the ones they like best in their own picture writing.

Allow time for children to share their messages and to try reading each other's picture writing. They can also write the English "translations" under each line of picture writing.

SESSION 4: "Bee! I'm Expecting You!"

INTRODUCTION

Introduce the session by telling students that the poem they are going to hear is a letter written to a bee by a friend. (Let children be surprised to discover at the end of the poem that the friend is a fly.)

FIRST READING

Ask children to listen as you read the poem aloud. Before reading the poem a second time, take a few moments to let children ask questions and make comments, and clear up unfamiliar vocabulary.

SECOND READING AND DISCUSSION

Read the poem a second time, encouraging students to follow along in their books and to join in saying the phrases "Bee! I'm expecting you!" and "Or better, be with me—/Yours, Fly."

After the reading, briefly review with students things that bees and flies have in common. Then help students think about the friendship between the fly and the bee in this poem by asking such questions as *The fly says he was talking yesterday to somebody the bee knows—who could that be? Why does the fly say the frogs are at work? What is the frogs' job? Why is the fly so eager for the bee to come back?*

GROUP CREATIVE WRITING AND ART ACTIVITY

Tell students that they are going to write the bee's reply to the fly's letter by thinking about some of the things the bee would look forward to doing with the fly when she returns. Write students' suggestions on the board as they offer them. You may want to help students get ideas by asking such questions as *When the bee and the fly get together, will they mostly work or play? Will the bee and the fly do anything special, or just be together? Will they do things by themselves, or with other creatures?*

Then have students turn to the page with the heading "Dear Fly." Ask them to write their own letters from the bee or to copy their favorite lines from the board.

After students have finished writing, they can illustrate the page by drawing what they think the fly and the bee will do when they get together. Allow time for children to share and compare their drawings.

SECRET MESSAGES

POETRY

What the Soldier Sees

THE DUMB SOLDIER

dumb: unable to speak

When the grass was closely mown,
Walking on the lawn alone,
In the turf a hole I found
And hid a soldier underground.

Spring and daisies came apace;

apace: quickly

Grasses hide my hiding-place;
Grasses run like a green sea
O'er the lawn up to my knee.

Under grass alone he lies,
Looking up with leaden eyes,
Scarlet coat and pointed gun,
To the stars and to the sun.

scythe is stoned:
grass-cutting tool is
sharpened

When the grass is ripe like grain,

When the scythe is stoned again,

When the lawn is shaven clear,

Then my hole shall reappear.

I shall find him, never fear,

I shall find my grenadier;

But for all that's gone and come,

I shall find my soldier dumb.

Why do you think
the boy hides his
soldier in the
ground?

*Why is the boy so sure he will
find his soldier again?*

52

He has lived, a little thing,
In the grassy woods of spring;
Done, if he could tell me true,
Just as I should like to do.

He has seen the starry hours
And the springing of the flowers;
And the fairy things that pass
In the forests of the grass.

In the silence he has heard
Talking bee and ladybird,
And the butterfly has flown
O'er him as he lay alone.

Not a word will he disclose,
Not a word of all he knows.
I must lay him on the shelf,
And make up the tale myself.

—Robert Louis Stevenson

disclose: reveal;
tell a secret

Why doesn't the boy mind losing his soldier for the whole spring and summer?

Why does the boy hide only one toy soldier? Why does he want the soldier to be alone?

Why would the boy like to live in the grass, like his soldier?

I would like to see _____

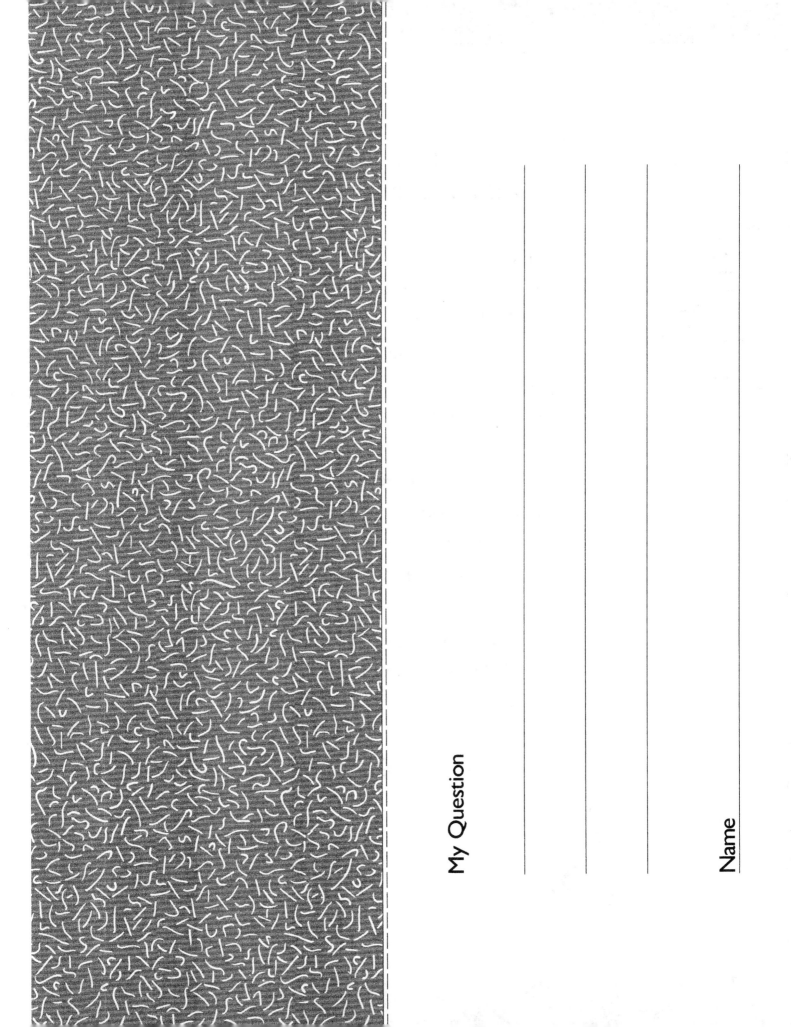

My Question _____

_____

_____

_____

Name

SNOW PRINT TWO:
HIEROGLYPHICS

In the alley
under the last cold rung
of the fire escape
birds are printing
the new snow
with a narrow alphabet.

Their scribbled secrets
tell of lost songs
and the howling wind
that claws like a cat.

These are messages
from the small dark birds
to me.

—Barbara Juster Esbensen

Messages From a Bird

1. _____

   _____

2. _____

   _____

3. _____

   _____

BEE! I'M EXPECTING YOU!

Bee! I'm expecting you!
Was saying Yesterday
To Somebody you know
That you were due—

The Frogs got Home last Week—
Are settled, and at work—
Birds, mostly back—
The Clover warm and thick—

You'll get my Letter by
The seventeenth; Reply
Or better, be with me—
Yours, Fly.

—Emily Dickinson

Dear Fly,

_____

_____

_____

_____

Yours,

Bee

A NOTE ABOUT THE READ-ALOUD SELECTIONS

The stories and poems in the Read-Aloud program are of the same high quality as all Junior Great Books selections. To ensure that selections will repay the sustained attention they receive in the program, and will hold children's interest for an extended period of time, all have passed through a stringent and lengthy review process.

First and foremost, selections in the Read-Aloud program must be emotionally compelling and imaginatively engaging. In order for children to develop a love of reading, they must be exposed to literature that speaks to their feelings and experience. Stories that strike a profound chord in children help them learn that reading is more than a basic processing of information; it is an inexhaustible source of pleasure and insight.

The Read-Aloud selections must also be well-written, conveying to children the delights of the written word. Through vivid language and strong, evocative images, children can have fun with reading. They soon discover that words contain meaning and associations that can be explored, played with, and savored.

Finally, selections are tested to ensure they embody interpretive ideas and themes that both children and adults find meaningful. When works are rich in meaning, children feel their efforts to read and understand them are rewarded. As children work with the stories and poems, they develop confidence in their own perceptions, and they become motivated to learn to read for themselves. Moreover, selections that have as much meaning for adults as for children help ensure that Shared Inquiry will be a collaborative effort among teachers, parents, and children.

Like the Junior Great Books program for older students, the Read-Aloud program features literature from a variety of cultures, including Native American, Caribbean, Asian, European, and African. Each selection embodies universal themes that all children can readily embrace—themes such as fairness, friendship, growing up, and learning about people and nature. By pursuing these themes with classmates in the Shared Inquiry environment, children gain experience in exploring their own unique perspectives and enlarging their understanding of ideas common to the human experience.

THE JUNIOR GREAT BOOKS READ-ALOUD SERIES

DRAGON SERIES

Volume I

The Frog Prince
   Brothers Grimm as told by Wanda Gág

Guinea Fowl and Rabbit Get Justice
   African folktale as told by Harold Courlander
   and George Herzog

"Nature Speaks"
   Poetry by Carl Sandburg, James Reeves,
   and Federico García Lorca

Volume 2

Feraj and the Magic Lute
   Arabian folktale as told by Jean Russell Larson

The Tale of Johnny Town-Mouse
   Beatrix Potter

"Companions"
   Poetry by A. A. Milne, Gwendolyn Brooks,
   and Robert Louis Stevenson

Volume 3

Buya Marries the Tortoise
   African folktale as told by W. F. P. Burton

The Huckabuck Family and How They Raised Pop
Corn in Nebraska and Quit and Came Back
   Carl Sandburg

"Magical Places"
   Poetry by Byrd Baylor, William Shakespeare,
   and Martin Brennan

SAILING SHIP SERIES

Volume I

The Shoemaker and the Elves
   Brothers Grimm as told by Wanda Gág

The Frog Went A-Traveling
   Russian folktale as told by Vsevolod Garshin

"Night into Dawn"
   Poetry by Robert Hillyer and John Ciardi,
   and a Mescalero Apache song

Volume 2

The Tale of Two Bad Mice
   Beatrix Potter

Bouki Cuts Wood
   Haitian folktale as told by Harold Courlander

"Fantasy"
   Poetry by Sylvia Plath, Edward Lear,
   and Lewis Carroll

Volume 3

Lion at School
   Philippa Pearce

Coyote Rides the Sun
   Native American folktale as told by
   Jane Louise Curry

"Seasons"
   Poetry by Nikki Giovanni, Langston Hughes,
   and Robert Louis Stevenson

THE JUNIOR GREAT BOOKS READ-ALOUD SERIES

SUN SERIES

Volume 1

The Black Hen's Egg
French folktale as told by
Natalie Savage Carlson

The Mouse and the Wizard
Hindu fable as told by Lucia Turnbull

"Imagination"
Poetry by Leslie Norris, Mark Van Doren,
and Robert Louis Stevenson

Volume 2

Rumpelstiltskin
Brothers Grimm, translated by Ralph Manheim

Eeyore Has a Birthday and Gets Two Presents
A. A. Milne

"When I Grow Up"
Poetry by Rabindranath Tagore and X. J. Kennedy,
and a Chippewa song

Volume 3

The King of the Frogs
African folktale as told by Humphrey Harman

Snow-White and the Seven Dwarfs
Brothers Grimm, translated by Randall Jarrell

"Mysterious Animals"
Poetry by T. S. Eliot, Jenifer Kelly,
and Robert Graves

PEGASUS SERIES

Volume 1

Chestnut Pudding
Iroquois folktale as told by John Bierhorst

The Pied Piper
English folktale as told by Joseph Jacobs

"Fanciful Animals"
Poetry by Edward Lear and A. A. Milne

Volume 2

The Mermaid Who Lost Her Comb
Scottish folktale as told by Winifred Finlay

Hansel and Gretel
Brothers Grimm, translated by Randall Jarrell

"Special Places"
Poetry by Gwendolyn Brooks and Robert Frost,
and a Navajo poem

Volume 3

Mother of the Waters
Haitian folktale as told by Diane Wolkstein

Zlateh the Goat
Isaac Bashevis Singer

"Secret Messages"
Poetry by Robert Louis Stevenson,
Barbara Juster Esbensen, and Emily Dickinson

SAMPLE LETTERS TO PARENTS
LETTER #1: To be sent home before the program begins

Dear Parents:

Our class will soon begin a new activity, an interpretive reading and discussion program called the Junior Great Books Read-Aloud program. Each week in this program, I will read an outstanding story or group of poems to the class and lead students in discussions, dramatizations, creative writing, and art projects. The program's structure offers children ongoing opportunities to develop their ideas about a challenging work of literature and to share those ideas with others.

The Read-Aloud program stresses the enjoyment of literature for its own sake, while at the same time it develops comprehension, interpretive thinking, and oral and written language skills. By listening to and reflecting on works that are rich in meaning, children feel that their efforts at understanding are rewarded, and they become more motivated to learn to read for themselves.

One evening a week, I will ask you to join in the program. Your child will bring home his or her book so that you can read aloud the selection for the week. Included in the book are a few questions for your child to answer as he or she thinks best. These questions (printed inside boxes and signaled by the character "G.B.") are open-ended questions that have no one "right" answer. Sometimes you will be asked to help your child underline or circle something on the page. But mostly you will be listening to your child talk about his or her answers. While relaxed and fun, this at-home work is important because it will form the basis of your child's work with the selection in class for the rest of the week.

At the end of the selection, there is a space for you to write down your child's own question about the story or poem. This question will be posted on a bulletin board with those of the rest of the class; these questions will then be shared and discussed during the week.

Our first at-home session will be _____. Please plan to set aside about one half-hour with your child on _____ evenings for the next _____ weeks. I'm sure you and your child will find the Junior Great Books Read-Aloud program an enjoyable and rewarding experience.

If you are interested in assisting me with the Read-Aloud program in the classroom, please contact me at the following number: _____. If you have had past experience leading a Junior Great Books group, or would like to take the special training course, you could help me conduct the activities, such as reading selections aloud to the children or leading Sharing Questions Discussions. I am also looking for parents who would like to prepare Read-Aloud bulletin boards, help students write captions during art activities, or assist in some other way. I would be happy to hear from you.

Sincerely,

LETTER #2: To be sent home at the time of the first at-home reading

Dear Parents:

Your child is bringing home his or her Read-Aloud book tonight. This book will be sent home on a regular basis for the rest of the term. The children will be using their books in class during the week, so please make sure your child brings the book back to school the very next day. The Read-Aloud books will be your child's to keep.

Your child can tell you which story or poem to read, since we read it in class today. As your child's at-home partner, you will read the selection aloud, ask G.B.'s questions (printed in the boxes), and write down your child's own question about the selection. The only other writing you are required to do is to help your child circle or underline on the page when the directions say to do so. (See the brief instructions at the front of your child's Read-Aloud book.) *Please note that the rest of the writing assignments and all of the drawing activities will be completed in class.*

The main thing to keep in mind as you read and talk with your child is to enjoy yourselves! This is an opportunity for your child to talk and ask questions about the selection in an intimate setting. Remember that these questions have no single right answer, and that this is just the beginning of your child's work with the selection. Answers shouldn't be considered final. One way to help your child fully express his or her ideas is to follow up a statement by asking, "Why do you think this?" or, "Can you tell me more?"

Your curiosity about what your child is thinking and the example you set as a good listener will communicate a very important message about the value of discussing ideas and the importance of reading for meaning. The role you fill in the Read-Aloud program is a vital one.

Sincerely,

TEACHER'S PRESENTATION OF THE READ-ALOUD PROGRAM TO PARENTS

This semester I will be using an exciting reading and discussion program called the Junior Great Books Read-Aloud program. It may be new to you. I would like to tell you about it because I believe it will make a big difference in your child's attitude toward reading, and in the way he or she approaches problem solving in general.

The Junior Great Books Read-Aloud program is just what its name suggests. It is a program in which I will read aloud to your children challenging works of literature—folktales, modern children's classics, and distinguished children's poetry. You, too, will have a chance to read the selections aloud to your child and discuss them with him or her.

We have chosen to include this program in your children's curriculum because it will help them learn to ask questions and share answers about the *meaning* of a story or poem. Over the course of a week, the children will hear a selection read several times and will work with it through a variety of drawing, writing, and oral activities. The one element common to all of these activities is the sharing of ideas through discussion.

In this program, your children will exercise the whole range of oral and written language skills needed to become good readers. Because much of the Read-Aloud work is done in groups, the children will learn how to work together to unlock the rich meaning of good stories and poems. Equally important, they will acquire a sense of confidence about being able to figure out for themselves what at first seems puzzling or too difficult. We expect that these attitudes will carry over to their other schoolwork. I look forward to seeing the children become better able to raise thoughtful questions and listen to others' ideas, whether the subject is science, social studies, math, or literature.

THE READ-ALOUD CLASSROOM ROUTINE

This is what the children's Read-Aloud books look like. *[Display a copy.]* As you can see, there are places throughout the book for the children to respond to each selection through drawing and writing activities. *[Point out some of the blank activity pages.]* When the children are finished working with the stories and poems in a book, the book is theirs to keep. As a permanent record of your child's unique interpretation of the stories and poems, each book will be something to share proudly with you.

Now that you have had a glimpse of the books used in the Read-Aloud program, I would like to review briefly what a typical week's work on a story, or small group of poems, will be like. By doing so, I'll also be able to give you a better idea of where you fit into the program.

The First Reading of the Story

Usually, we will spend an entire week on a single story or small group of poems. This unhurried pace will give all the children an opportunity to show their strengths and discover new ones. A typical week begins with my reading a story or poem aloud to the children, after which they complete an assigned drawing that allows them to record their early responses to the selection. For example, after listening to the first reading of "Rumpelstiltskin," the children will be asked to draw what they think is the best or worst thing that happens to the miller's daughter during her first night at the king's palace. They might choose to illustrate the moment when the king commands her to spin the straw into gold; the point in the story where she gives in to her fear and sorrow at being locked in the room filled with straw, and begins to weep; or the sight of Rumpelstiltskin magically spinning the straw for her. In choosing what to illustrate, the children are visualizing the characters and setting of the story. And as they make their own decisions about what the best or worst thing is, they are learning that their individual perspectives on the story are important.

The At-Home Session

The second reading of the selection, which takes place at home with you or another adult partner, comes next. When reading the story aloud, you will want to encourage your child to follow along when possible and to repeat or join in saying any underlined words or phrases. You will also pause during your reading to ask several open-ended questions printed in the margin of the book. As you will note *[hold up book and display an example],* these questions are "boxed," and they are always accompanied by the Read-Aloud mascot, "G.B." (Incidentally, G.B.'s initials come from the name of the program—*Great Books.*) When discussing G.B.'s questions, you will want to keep in mind that there is no one "right" answer. These questions will be discussed again in class, at which time your child will have a chance to offer his or her ideas and to listen and respond to the thoughts of others.

The important thing for you to remember is that answers should never be considered final. Because this at-home session is a time for cozy, one-on-one work, you should encourage your children to take their time when they express their ideas. Also, help clear up any misunderstandings they might have about the facts of the story. At the end of the session, you will write—or help your child write—his or her own question about the selection into the book. *[Display "My Question" space.]* The next day, all the children's questions will be posted on a bulletin board, to be shared and discussed throughout the rest of the week.

The Third Reading of the Story and Discussion of the At-Home Work

All of the remaining work on a selection is completed in class. (This includes filling in the rest of the blank spaces in the book designated for writing or drawing.) During our second in-class session, I will read the selection aloud for the third time and, as I mentioned before, the class will talk about their answers to the questions discussed at home the previous night. This in-class discussion gives the children another opportunity to add to, or revise, their thinking about the selection. This session usually ends with a dramatization or an art activity based on the issues explored in the children's at-home work.

The Remaining Sessions

The remaining two sessions include writing activities, a group discussion of the selection, and additional dramatizations and art activities. The group discussion of the selection is a very important activity. It is based on five or six thought-provoking questions I have about the selection, and it includes, whenever possible, questions that the children produced during their at-home session. For example, a discussion of "Rumpelstiltskin" might be based on such questions as "Why does the miller try to impress the king by saying his daughter can spin straw into gold?" and "Why does Rumpelstiltskin demand payment for his help when he can spin as much gold as he wants?"

THE DRAMATIZATION, ART, AND WRITING ACTIVITIES

All of the dramatization, art, and writing activities in the Read-Aloud program help the children think more deeply about a selection. Early in a unit, a dramatization might help the children get the details of a story's plot straight. But dramatizations also help them interpret a story, as they think about what a character is feeling or thinking, and about why that character says or does something. For example, the dramatization activity for "Snow-White and the Seven Dwarfs" will have the children act out the three scenes in which the Queen tricks Snow-White with the laces, the poisoned comb, and the poisoned apple. In this way, the children will have an opportunity to examine the Queen's character more closely, as well as explore her relationship with the innocent Snow-White. After the dramatization, the children will write answers to the interpretive question "Why does Snow-White let herself be fooled by the wicked Queen?" They will then share and discuss their answers.

The art activities your child completes in the Read-Aloud book will be a visual record of his or her interpretation of different aspects of each story or poem. When you first examine your child's book, you will probably be struck by the fact that there are few professional illustrations, and that those few are done in black and white. This design was chosen because your child will be the chief illustrator of the book. Your child's drawings will reflect his or her own ideas about what a character is like, what the mood of a story or poem is, or why something happens. For example, a drawing assignment for "The Pied Piper" is preceded by a discussion in which children think about the Pied Piper's character: Is he greedy, fair, mean, fun, scary, magical, or smart? After the children have thought and talked about what words they each would use to describe the Pied Piper, they will draw a picture of him showing what kind of person they think he is. Naturally, each child's picture will be different, reflecting his or her individual ideas about this character and, by extension, about the story as a whole. Usually, the art activities will end with the children sharing their drawings with the class, so that they have a chance to explain why they made their pictures as they did.

There will be many opportunities for the children to write in the Read-Aloud program. The writing activities for a single selection come in a variety of forms. Some activities are completed independently, with the children dictating to me when necessary, while others are "written" orally as a group. Some compositions are very brief, such as the questions the children write during the at-home session and the captions that they write in class for their drawings. The children will also write or dictate answers to thought-provoking questions about a selection. Finally, there are the creative-writing activities, such as the group writing assignment the class will complete for the "Rumpelstiltskin" unit. This activity asks the children to write a paragraph describing the inside of Rumpelstiltskin's hut. Scheduled at the end of the week's work on the story, this activity builds on the children's interpretations of Rumpelstiltskin, for in describing Rumpelstiltskin's hut they are indirectly describing his character. It also gives the children an opportunity to exercise their imaginations by inventing details about Rumpelstiltskin's belongings.

CONCLUSION

As I have tried to indicate in this short talk, the benefits of the Read-Aloud program will, I believe, prove to be far-reaching. At the same time that your children are learning about oral and written language, they will be discovering the excitement and satisfaction of critical thinking.

As the adult partner for the at-home session, you will have an ideal opportunity to encourage your child in this all-important endeavor. Your active interest in what your child is thinking about a selection will communicate a vital message to him or her about the importance of discussing ideas and the value of reading.

If any of you are interested in assisting me with the Read-Aloud program in the classroom, please let me know. If you have past experience leading Junior Great Books groups, or would like to take the special training course, you might consider helping me conduct the activities, such as reading the selections aloud to the children or leading the group discussion of a story or poem. I am also looking for parents who would like to prepare Read-Aloud bulletin boards, help students writing captions during the art activities, or assist in some other way.

Suggested handouts:

Photocopies of Appendix A, "A Note About the Read-Aloud Selections"

Photocopies of samples of student work from completed Read-Aloud books (if available)

READINGS AND TOPICS FOR AN INTEGRATED CURRICULUM

Chestnut Pudding

Literature

Native American tales:

Baylor, Byrd, comp. *And It Is Still That Way: Legends Told by Arizona Indian Children.* Scribner's, 1976.

Bierhorst, John. *The Naked Bear: Folktales of the Iroquois.* Morrow, 1987.

———. *The Red Swan: Myths and Tales of the American Indians.* Farrar, 1976.

Courlander, Harold. *People of the Short Blue Corn: Tales and Legends of the Hopi Indians.* Illustrated by Enrico Arno. Harcourt, 1970.

Erdoes, Richard, ed. *The Sound of Flutes and Other Indian Legends.* Illustrated by Paul Goble. Pantheon, 1976.

Fritz, Jean. *The Good Giants and the Bad Pukwudgies.* Illustrated by Tomie dePaola. Putnam, 1982.

Goble, Paul. *Buffalo Woman.* Illustrated by the author. Bradbury, 1984.

———, ad. *Star Boy.* Illustrated by the adapter. Bradbury, 1983.

Grinnell, George Bird, comp. *The Whistling Skeleton: American Indian Tales of the Supernatural.* Edited by John Bierhorst. Four Winds, 1982.

Harris, Christie. *Once Upon a Totem.* Illustrated by John Frazer Mills. Atheneum, 1963.

McDermott, Gerald, ad. *Arrow to the Sun: A Pueblo Indian Tale.* Illustrated by the adapter. Viking, 1974.

Macmillan, Cyrus. *Glooskap's Country, and Other Indian Tales.* Illustrated by John A. Hall. Walck, 1956.

Reid, Dorothy N. *Tales of Nanabozhoo.* Illustrated by Donald Grant. Walck, 1963.

Retellings of the "Sorcerer's Apprentice" legend:

Gág, Wanda, and Tomes, Margot. *The Sorcerer's Apprentice.* Coward, 1979.

Mayer, Marianna. *The Sorcerer's Apprentice: A Greek Fable.* Bantam, 1989.

Social Studies

Chestnuts: A Staple Food in Ancient Times
The Everyday Life of the Iroquois People

Science

Moles
The Life Cycle of Chestnut Trees
How Gorges Are Formed

Math

Word Problems *(based on chestnuts or on the animals the boy encounters during his quest)*

The Pied Piper

Literature

Browning, Robert. *The Pied Piper of Hamelin.* Illustrated by Kate Greenaway. Warne, 1979.

Jacobs, Joseph. *English Fairy Tales.* Dover, 1967.

_____. *More English Fairy Tales.* Schocken, 1968.

_____. *The Pied Piper and Other Tales.* Illustrated by James Hill. Macmillan, 1963.

Steel, Flora Annie. *English Fairy Tales.* Illustrated by Arthur Rackham. Macmillan, 1918, 1979.

Social Studies

Life in a Medieval Town (including the songs and games of children)
Early Flute (Pipe) Music: The Songs of Traveling Minstrels

Science

The Colors of the Rainbow

Math

Money *(have students "higgle and haggle" over the prices of things)*

"Fanciful Animals"

Literature

Poetry by Edward Lear (selected bibliography):

> *The Complete Nonsense of Edward Lear.* Dover, n.d.
>
> *The Jumblies.* Illustrated by Edward Gorey. W. R. Scott, 1968.
>
> *The Owl and the Pussy-Cat.* Illustrated by William Pène du Bois. Doubleday, 1962.
>
> *The Quangle Wangle's Hat.* Illustrated by Helen Oxenbury. Watts, 1969.
>
> *The Scroobious Pip.* Completed by Ogden Nash. Illustrated by Nancy Ekholm Burkert. Harper, 1968.
>
> *Whizz!* Illustrated by Janina Domanska. Macmillan, 1973.

Poetry by A. A. Milne:

> *Now We Are Six.* Illustrated by Ernest Shepard. Dutton, 1927.
>
> *When We Were Very Young.* Illustrated by Ernest Shepard. Dutton, 1924.

Social Studies

The History of Teddy Bears

Wedding Traditions Around the World

Kings and Queens of France *(show what they looked like)*

Science

Characteristics and Habitats of Birds in the Lear Poems (stork, duck, owl, canary, grouse, and turkey)

Math

Measurement: How Long Is a Foot? How Long Is 102 Feet? (the width of the Quangle Wangle's hat)

Hansel and Gretel

Literature

Illustrated editions of "Hansel and Gretel":

> Illustrated by Adrienne Adams. Translated by Charles Scribner. Scribner's, 1975.
>
> Illustrated and adapted by Anthony Browne. Julia MacRae Books, 1981.
>
> Illustrated by Paul O. Zelinsky. Retold by Rika Lesser. Dodd, 1984.
>
> Illustrated by Lisbeth Zwerger. Translated by Elizabeth Crawford. Morrow, 1980.

Illustrated editions of tales by Jacob and Wilhelm Grimm:

> *About Wise Men and Simpletons: Twelve Tales from Grimm.* Illustrated by Nonny Hogrogian. Translated by Elizabeth Shub. Macmillan, 1971.
>
> *The Brothers Grimm: Popular Folk Tales.* Illustrated by Michael Foreman. Translated by Brian Alderson. Gollancz, 1978.
>
> *Grimm's Fairy Tales: Twenty Stories.* Illustrated by Arthur Rackham. Viking, 1973.
>
> *Household Stories by the Brothers Grimm.* Illustrated by Walter Crane. Translated by Lucy Crane. Dover, 1963.
>
> *More Tales from Grimm.* Freely translated and illustrated by Wanda Gág. Coward, 1947.
>
> *Rare Treasures from Grimm: Fifteen Little Known Tales.* Illustrated by Erik Blegvad. Compiled and translated by Ralph Manheim. Doubleday, 1981.
>
> *Tales from Grimm.* Freely translated and illustrated by Wanda Gág. Coward, 1936.

Social Studies

Compare "Hansel and Gretel" to similar tales from other cultures (listed below):

Afanasyev, Aleksandr. "The Grumbling Old Woman." In *Russian Fairy Tales*, translated by Norbert Guterman. Pantheon, 1945.

Calvino, Italo. "Chick." In *Italian Folktales*, translated by George Martin. Pantheon, 1980.

"The Deserted Children" (Native American). In *Best-Loved Folktales of the World*, edited by Joanna Cole. Doubleday, 1982.

"Kadar and Cannibals." In *South Indian Folktales of Kadar*, edited by Zacharias P. Thundy. Folklore Institute (India), 1983.

"The Lost Children." In *The Borzoi Book of French Folk Tales*, edited by Paul Delarue and translated by Austin E. Fife. Knopf, 1956.

Seki, Keigo. "The Oni and the Three Children." In *Folktales of Japan*, translated by Robert J. Adams. University of Chicago Press, 1963.

Science

Products of the Forest

Math

Make a gingerbread house *(measure ingredients; learn about baking temperatures; assemble pieces of different shapes and sizes)*

The Mermaid Who Lost Her Comb

Literature

Scottish/Celtic tales:

    Finlay, Winifred. *Folk Tales from Moor and Mountain.* Roy Publishers, 1969.

    Jacobs, Joseph, ed. *Celtic Fairy Tales* and *More Celtic Fairy Tales.* Dover, 1968.

    Manning-Sanders, Ruth. *Scottish Folk Tales.* Illustrated by William Stobbs. Methuen, 1982.

    ————. *Stories from the English and Scottish Ballads.* Dutton, 1968.

    Nic Leodhas, Sorche. *Always Room for One More.* Illustrated by Nonny Hogrogian. Holt, 1965.

    ————. *By Loch and by Lin.* Illustrated by Vera Bock. Holt, 1969.

    ————. *Claymore and Kilt.* Illustrated by Leo and Diane Dillon. Holt, 1967.

    ————. *Heather and Broom.* Illustrated by Consuelo Joerns. Holt, 1960.

See also:

    Jarrell, Randall. *The Animal Family.* Dell, 1965. A lonely hunter forms a family with a mermaid.

Social Studies

Life Along the Coast of Scotland

The Mermaid Legend in Different Cultures

Science

Seashells

Seals

Math

Rudimentary Division Problems *(based on the boy breaking the razor shell while carving it)*

"Special Places"

Literature

Native American poetry:

Allen, Terry, ed. *The Whispering Wind.* Doubleday, 1972.

Bierhorst, John, ed. *In the Trail of the Wind.* Farrar, 1971.

————. *The Sacred Path: Spells, Prayers, and Power Songs of the American Indians.* Morrow, 1983.

Brandon, William, ed. *The Magic World: American Indian Songs and Poems.* Morrow, 1971.

Clymer, Theodore, ed. *Four Corners of the Sky: Poems, Chants, and Oratory.* Illustrated by Marc Brown. Little, 1975.

Houston, James, ed. *Songs of the Dream People.* Illustrated by the author. Atheneum, 1972.

Jones, Hettie, ed. *The Trees Stand Shining: Poetry of the North American Indians.* Illustrated by Robert Andrew Parker. Dial, 1971.

Sneve, Virginia Driving Hawk, ed. *Dancing Teepees: Poems of American Indian Youth.* Holiday, 1989.

Wetherill, Hilda Faunce. *Navajo Indian Poems.* Vantage, 1952.

See also:

Brooks, Gwendolyn. *Bronzeville Boys and Girls.* Illustrated by Ronni Solbert. Harper, 1956.

Frost, Robert. *A Swinger of Birches.* Illustrated by Peter Koeppen. Stemmer House, 1982.

————. *You Come Too.* Holt, 1964.

Social Studies

Navajo Culture (emphasize sheep herding, the steps of wool processing, and weaving)

Different Jobs Dogs Do (herding, seeing eye, police, etc.)

Science

Dairy Farming: How Cows Produce Milk

Math

Counting *(determine the age of a tree by counting its rings)*

Mother of the Waters

Literature

Books by Diane Wolkstein (selected bibliography):

Lazy Stories. Seabury, 1976.

The Magic Orange Tree and Other Haitian Folktales. Illustrated by Elsa Henriquez. Knopf, 1978.

The Magic Wings: A Tale From China. Dutton, 1983.

White Wave: A Chinese Tale. T. Crowell, 1979.

Caribbean literature:

Agard, John. *Say It Again, Granny! Twenty Poems from Caribbean Proverbs.* Illustrated by Susanna Gretz. Bodley Head, 1986.

Berry, James. *Spiderman Anancy.* Holt, 1988.

Courlander, Harold. *The Piece of Fire and Other Haitian Folktales.* Harcourt, 1964.

Sherlock, Philip. *Anansi, the Spider Man: Jamaican Folk Tales.* Illustrated by Marcia Brown. T. Crowell, 1954.

_____. *The Iguana's Tail: Crick Crack Stories from the Caribbean.* T. Crowell, 1969.

_____. *West Indian Folk Tales.* Oxford University Press, 1988.

Sherlock, Philip and Hilary. *Ears and Tails and Common Sense.* T. Crowell, 1974.

Social Studies

The People and Geography of Haiti

The Four Directions: North, South, East, and West *(use the "crossroads" to demonstrate)*

Science

Folk Medicine: The Uses of Healing Herbs and Roots

Math

Weight and Measurement *(weigh or measure foods mentioned in the story, such as rice, beans, and bananas)*

Zlateh the Goat

Literature

Books by Isaac Bashevis Singer (selected bibliography):

The Fools of Chelm and Their History. Translated by Elizabeth Shub. Illustrated by Uri Shulevitz. Farrar, 1973.

Stories for Children. Farrar, 1984.

When Shlemiel Went to Warsaw and Other Stories. Translated by the author and Elizabeth Shub. Illustrated by Margot Zemach. Dell, 1968.

See also:

Aleichem, Sholem. *Hanukah Money.* Illustrated by Uri Shulevitz. Greenwillow, 1978.

Weinreich, Beatrice, ed. *Yiddish Folktales.* Translated by Leonard Wolf. Pantheon, 1988.

Social Studies

How Hanukkah Is Celebrated in Different Lands

Science

The Insulating Power of Snow (igloos)

Math

Play the game dreidel (instructions below)

A dreidel is a small top with four sides, each marked with a Hebrew letter. The four letters commemorate Hanukkah by forming the acronym for "A great miracle happened there." You can purchase a dreidel inexpensively at a synagogue gift shop or Jewish bookstore. Or, you can make one by drilling a hole through the center of a small wood block and inserting a wooden skewer through the hole.

To play dreidel, place a "kitty" of counters, pennies, nuts, or candies in the center of the group. Children then take turns spinning the dreidel and either taking from or paying back the kitty, according to the letter that lands face up:

נ   ("nun")—player neither takes nor gives anything;

ג   ("gimmel")—player puts one into the kitty;

ה   ("hay")—player takes half the kitty;

ש   ("shin")—player puts all his winnings back into the kitty.

Play is over after a predetermined number of rounds have been finished, or when one player has won all of the kitty.

"Secret Messages"

Literature

Illustrated editions of Robert Louis Stevenson's *A Child's Garden of Verses:*
    Illustrated by Jessie Willcox Smith. Scribner's, 1905, 1969.
    Illustrated by Tasha Tudor. Walck, 1947.
    Illustrated by Brian Wildsmith. Watts, 1966.

Works for children by Emily Dickinson (selected bibliography):
    I'm Nobody! Who Are You? Illustrated by Rex Schneider. Stemmer House, 1978.
    Letter to the World. Edited by Rumer Godden. Illustrated by Prudence Seward. Macmillan, 1969.
    Poems. Edited by Helen Plotz. Illustrated by Robert Kipness. T. Crowell, 1964.

Social Studies

Alphabets of Different Peoples (hieroglyphics, cuneiform, Arabic, Hebrew,
    Cyrillic, Chinese and Japanese characters)
The History of Toy Soldiers

Science

Bees and How They Make Honey
How Different Species of Birds Live During the Winter

Math

Codes and Ciphers *(assign a number to each letter of the alphabet and have
    students write secret messages using the number code)*
Geometric Shapes *(use a bee's honeycomb to illustrate a hexagon)*

Acknowledgments

All possible care has been taken to trace ownership and secure permission for each selection in this series. The Great Books Foundation wishes to thank the following authors, publishers, and representatives for permission to reprint copyrighted material:

Chestnut Pudding, from THE NAKED BEAR: FOLKTALES OF THE IROQUOIS, by John Bierhorst. Copyright 1987 by John Bierhorst. Reprinted by permission of William Morrow & Co.

"Teddy Bear," from WHEN WE WERE VERY YOUNG, by A. A. Milne. Copyright 1924 by E. P. Dutton; renewed 1952 by A. A. Milne. Reprinted by permission of Dutton Children's Books, a division of Penguin Books USA, Inc.

The Mermaid Who Lost Her Comb, from FOLK TALES FROM MOOR AND MOUNTAIN, by Winifred Finlay. Copyright 1969 by Winifred Finlay. First published in *Child Education* magazine, Scholastic Publications. Reprinted by permission of *Child Education.*

Hansel and Gretel, from THE GOLDEN BIRD AND OTHER TALES FROM THE BROTHERS GRIMM, translated by Randall Jarrell. Copyright 1963 by Macmillan Publishing Company. Reprinted by permission of Macmillan Publishing Company.

"Little Puppy," from NAVAJO INDIAN POEMS, by Hilda Faunce Wetherill.

"Lyle," from BRONZEVILLE BOYS AND GIRLS, by Gwendolyn Brooks. Copyright 1956 by Gwendolyn Brooks Blakely. Reprinted by permission of Harper & Row, Publishers, Inc.

"The Pasture," by Robert Frost, from THE POETRY OF ROBERT FROST, edited by Edward Connery Lathem. Copyright 1939, 1967, 1969 by Holt, Rinehart and Winston, Inc. Reprinted by permission of Henry Holt and Company, Inc.

Mother of the Waters, from THE MAGIC ORANGE TREE AND OTHER HAITIAN FOLKTALES, by Diane Wolkstein. Copyright 1978 by Diane Wolkstein. Reprinted by permission of Alfred A. Knopf, Inc.

Zlateh the Goat, from ZLATEH THE GOAT AND OTHER STORIES, by Isaac Bashevis Singer. Copyright 1966 by Isaac Bashevis Singer. Reprinted by permission of Harper & Row, Publishers, Inc.

"Snow Print Two: Hieroglyphics," from COLD STARS AND FIREFLIES: POEMS OF THE FOUR SEASONS, by Barbara Juster Esbensen. Copyright 1984 by Barbara Juster Esbensen. Reprinted by permission of Harper & Row, Publishers, Inc.

"Bee! I'm Expecting You!" from THE POEMS OF EMILY DICKINSON, edited by Thomas H. Johnson. Copyright 1951, 1955, 1979, 1983 by the President and Fellows of Harvard College. Reprinted by permission of the Belknap Press of Harvard University Press and the Trustees of Amherst College.

Illustration Credits

David Cunningham prepared the illustrations for *Chestnut Pudding*.

Michael Carroll prepared the illustrations for *The Pied Piper*.

Diane Cole prepared the illustrations for *"The Quangle Wangle's Hat"* and *"Little Puppy."*

Edward Lear's illustrations for *"The Owl and the Pussy-Cat"* were reproduced courtesy of the Newberry Library.

Ernest Shepard's illustrations for *"Teddy Bear"* are from WHEN WE WERE VERY YOUNG. Reprinted by permission of Dutton Children's Books, a division of Penguin Books USA, Inc. Reproduced courtesy of the Newberry Library. Illustration on page 60 by William Seabright.

Donna Diamond prepared the illustrations for *The Mermaid Who Lost Her Comb*.

Paul Hoffman prepared the illustrations for *Hansel and Gretel* and *"The Pasture."*

Mary Jones prepared the illustration for *"Lyle."*

Ralph Creasman prepared the illustrations for *Mother of the Waters*.

Emily Arnold McCully prepared the illustrations for *"Snow Print Two: Hieroglyphics"* and the border art for *Zlateh the Goat*.

Geoffrey Moss prepared the illustrations for *"The Dumb Soldier."*

"G.B." was created by Ed Young. Copyright 1990 by Ed Young.

Cover art by Rich Lo. Cover design by THINK Book Works.

Book design by William Seabright and Paul Uhl, Design Associates.